MY TRADING BIBLE

Also by
Mark Andrew Ritchie

God in the Pits;
Confessions of a Commodities Trader

Spirit of the Rainforest;
A Yanomamo Shaman's Story

Treasures of My Heart

The Last Shibboleth

for discounts on all titles visit

MarkRitchie.me

MY TRADING BIBLE

LOSE YOUR SHIRT, SAVE YOUR LIFE, CARRY ON TRADING

MARK ANDREW RITCHIE

**ISLAND
LAKE
PRESS**
ISLAND LAKE
ILLINOIS

ISBN: 978-0-9646952-0-7

Island Lake Press
Box 710
Island Lake, Illinois 60042

TABLE OF CONTENTS

INTRODUCTION

Allow a word of explanation. Originally this book had the title, "How to Lose a Fortune and Avoid Suicide." That explains why publishers insist on the right to the title. It also explains the direction of some of the content. While many of you could not deal with such a title, others of you have praised it. One person who had close experience with suicide said, "It's about time someone had the courage to use that word in a title." Nevertheless, the title has gone down with a thousand insults. But it has been recovered for the opening chapter. Alas, the publishers have creative control over the chapter titles as well. Marketing constraints are a reality. But the severity of our industry is also a reality. Regardless of the title, we will not overlook the theme.

The process you are beginning has required me to review almost forty years, if I leave out the gambling part. Quite by accident, and surprise, it is possible that I have stumbled across that elusive trait that makes a winning trader. Don't ask now. But to satisfy an ounce of your curiosity and start you thinking in the trader's direction, I'll mention what makes a losing trader. That would be the urge to learn what makes a winning trader in the intro and save the trouble of going through nine chapters. I am sorry—up front honesty is one of those indispensable traits.

Speaking of indispensable, whether a trader or not, one can use a support group. Steve Van Rooy not only began insisting on this book, but also did the "work" to assure its completion. "Where's that next chapter?" will ring in my ears for some time. Without his inflicted grief, you would not be reading this.

Actually, what snapped Van Rooy's encouragement into focus was an invitation from a fellow trader to speak at his seminar. I had never met Jim Prince and knew nothing of his trading style. He had sold my book to his clients, there was a built up curiosity, and their seminar that summer was scheduled for Chicago.

I asked him what he would like me to talk about. He said, "Your book has been very helpful, neatly packaged, highly theoretical. But it demands a public defense. Why don't you stand up, put up, or shut up?" Wait, before you report me to Prince, that is not exactly how he put it. He said, "We would be honored to have you come and say a few words." But what *I* heard was—that previous, "put-up-or-shut-up" line. A lot of commodity traders hear voices. We do our best to ignore them. When he added the info about the outing in the exclusive Sheffield Avenue rooftop overlooking the Cubs right field, this became a no-brainer speaking engagement.

What shocked me that week was the reaction of his audience. They acted like the material I presented was from another planet. The comment, "We've never heard anything like this before," is open to a wide variety of interpretations. Whether a compliment or not will be left to your discretion. At the very least it was a reminder of Van Rooy's call for me to get back to work.

And there were more: Tad Drew encouraged, edited, simulated covers, and generally stayed on my case until completion. If you are like me, get a friend who is not afraid to kick the posterior until you "git r done." And many thanks to everyone else—first my amazing woman (cf. chap 5 and back cover), Mark II for the last chapter, Peter Brandt for critique and encouragement, my cousin Dr. Kurt Free, Mike and Kathy Fisher, Annette Ross, Rick Cordell, Pamela Smotherman, the late Neil Knudsen, the late Larry Burkett, Prof Norman L. Geisler, and still after all these years, my inspirational class of '66.

CHAPTER ONE

HOW TO LOSE A FORTUNE AND AVOID SUICIDE

My wife longed for the five acres next to our house. Actually, we had already purchased the five acres on one side, but she wanted a little more space on the other side. Well, to be honest (honesty will rear its questionable head in this book), I wanted it just as badly; admittedly, all my places (Oregon, Texas, Afghanistan) had open spaces that didn't cost a fortune. We were slightly familiar with the land developer who sold us the lake front lot where we had built a few years earlier. Since we had bought the extra five acres on one side from him, we now intended to buy the other lot. I asked my real estate broker to make an offer, which he did. The developer countered with an extremely high price. One could have called it ridiculous. But you probably already know that one person's *ridiculous* is another person's value. However, values can change. If that is news, you have picked up the wrong book. Sometimes they change fast enough that *ridiculous* is the only word that applies.

So I ignored his counter offer and within a few days he gave my agent a lower counter. Now things got interesting. I countered his counter with an offer that was lower than my initial offer. I already told you, markets change. And BTW, these days we are the happy recipients of a class of real estate agents who refrain from telling us that real estate can't go down in value. But I can promise you that we have only a few more years to enjoy this state of enlightenment on their part.

The seller did not appreciate my lower offer. He countered at a number very close to my original offer and added, "That client of yours, Mark Ritchie, is a conniving Jew."[1]

I told my broker, "Take the offer, close the deal, and be sure to thank him for the compliment."

Now here is my goal for you readers: That you will become traders worthy of such a compliment.[2] And you may as well recall that the most famous Jew of all time taught us that we should be crafty as snakes and harmless as doves. Most of my Christian friends consume their spiritual capital trying to emulate the dove. Countless sermons have been delivered on the eternal reward that awaits the one who can humbly exemplify that bird, while a vacuum is left for the theology of the snake.

It is my intention to fill that vacuum. So while I am borrowing a theme from Jesus, I might as well mention early that it is my state of spiritual surety that got me into this book in the first place. About my first book, Kirkus Reviews wrote that Ritchie has the calm confidence of a Christian with four aces.[3] While this is not true, no professional trader will question that the one thing we need in this business is confidence, but in just the right amount. Every one of us professional traders can tell you a story of a trader, more sure of himself than the rest of us, who went down with a sure-thing trade. Then certainly after they liquidated his position, the market reversed and went exactly where he knew it would.

---

[1] I might as well deal with this point now because it will come up repeatedly. The one thing one gets out of this industry is stories that need no embellishment. So I affirm (in answer to your obvious question) that this story, and all the rest in this dialogue, are not only true, but free of even the minutest exaggeration.

[2] Lesson one: The insult (as well as the compliment) is open to varying interpretations. Try not to miss the complimentary side of it even if you have to massage the meaning. If that doesn't work, just consider the source.

[3] I wouldn't turn down a compliment, although I'm not sure how to interpret this one.

We will return often to this confidence theme. But first we need to divide ourselves into four groups. Then cover the excuses and other introductory details.

FOUR DISTINCT CLASSES OF READERS

Professional Traders

(five years in the black and 1000 trades)

Go ahead and skip to chapter four.[4] You bought this book for chapter four, maybe chapter five as well. So get on with it. I'll get your attention by calling it the holy grail, as unorthodox as it is to say that; we all know that there is no holy grail in our business; the search for it is a fool's time-waster. But I insist. You can return here for all the rest of the intermediate info that must lay the groundwork for good trading. I'll die of shock if there is anything new in these first three chapters. So speed on to chapter four and the rest of us will meet you there. I don't minimize this groundwork; it is indispensable for successful trading. But you will have no need for it.

Semi-professional Traders

(one year in the black and 100 trades)

Feel free to skim, skip, and overlook any section that does not apply as you hurry to follow those pros to chapters four and five. You'll soon see if you are getting ahead of yourself. Just be ready to return here to fill in the missing pieces.

---

[4] Don't you despise those books that are 95 percent fluff and 5 percent substance? And that 5 percent could be unnecessarily complimentary. So if you are a seasoned professional, skip to chapter 4 for the "holy grail" (or as close to it as this trader will come) and you'll have what you came for.

Beginners and Wannabes

(no need to check your total equity, you know who you are)

I can hear you, "Gimme entry and exit points that will turn my trading around! I'll take care of the rest." The "rest" is what you have overlooked. Continue reading from here and do not skip anything (except those closing FYX sections). It's that skipping ahead for the quick money that will get (or "has gotten") you in trouble. You must read everything and *do not* feel free to ignore the footnotes unless they are on a topic that is familiar to you. You never know when an important item, slightly off subject, could be in a footnote.[5] This is the only way to know if our industry is for you. If you simply trade until you can't any more, i.e., run out of money, you will have an ugly experience, put stress on all your interpersonal relationships, and prove the validity of the title of this chapter. Also, take seriously each invitation to "get another book," or to "go back to the beginning." It is not entry and exit points that you need; you are lacking a systematic game plan.

For You Christians (FYX)

The fourth class actually turns out to be a subset of any one of the previous three: Christians. Please permit me, for a moment, the inaccuracy of a quick generalization. You Christians (and I among you) fall into two camps.

First—to those who believe that holy writ, and the flowery What-Would-Jesus-Do questions, do not apply to the dog-eat-dog world of capitalism. Business is business. The clergy would surely agree if they had to compete in a world where one must buy low and sell high in order to feed the family. If

---

[5] Very good; here you are. One time a guy came up to me after a talk and said, "Your message is interesting enough, but it's your side comments, afterthoughts, and wise cracks that are the most informative." No self-respecting editor would allow all these rabbit trails into a text that is supposed to be moving forward. This compromise will save my editors hours of author-editor conflict. (They'll probably want that sentence out.) And this is why I have insisted that these cannot be endnotes. Endnotes are the reader's rabbit trail.

there's no crying in baseball, there certainly is no "turning the other cheek" in capitalism.

Second–those who would like to see a scripture verse to back up every truth claim. So at the end of each chapter there will be added the FYX section (For You Christians).[6] Over time, we trust that those in the first group will see that capitalism, free market enterprise, and Adam Smith's invisible hand are quite consistent with biblical truth. Indeed, many of the stories Jesus created, revealed a thorough familiarity with these concepts. If you are in that first group, give it time.

But for the rest of you, these sections will be a waste of your time, as I will be reminding you constantly. We Christians have some issues that the rest of you do not–some advantages, but also some disadvantages (which may be insurmountable). We struggle with the knowledge that our pastors are nervous and suspicious of speculators. They are conflicted concerning how much unrighteous mammon they can tolerate being placed in the offering plate. You'll catch the point soon enough.

INTRODUCTORY DETAILS (EXCUSES FOR ONE MORE BOOK)

Let me address a few important details at the outset. These will give you an overview of where this tutorial is headed.

Now that we have sent the pros and maybe the semi-pros on to chapter four, let's cover some introductory material. I've already guessed at what you want from me; buy points, sell points, and a few relevant hot tips from the floor. If you think our business is that simple, you've been listening to too many salacious cocktail party stories told by the smartest guy in the room. Save your money and find another book to read.

The money I want you to save is not the price of this book; that's pocket change–but thank-you very much. No, I'm referring to your life savings. That's what's in jeopardy. This is why my friends have been begging me not to write anything that

---

[6] Don't get offended by the X. It has always been used as an abbreviation for the Greek word Xristos (Christ, messiach), as in Xmas.

might encourage you to trade. In the past you've ignored my advice against trading ("rants," is what they really are). So now, at the very least, this will give you an honest evaluation of what you are up against. First let's review a number of details and excuses for yet another book about investing.

WHAT'S WITH THE FLIPPANT TITLE ABOUT SUICIDE?

One day I was interrupted by a call from a stranger, out of state, a pastor, who told my assistant that he "really needed to talk to me." He had gotten into trading to supplement his meager pastoral salary. Any trader can tell you where this story is going. He was in big financial trouble. After listening to his story for a few minutes, I said, "Well, first things first: Don't do anything stupid."

Naturally he asked, "Like what?"

I said, "Like taking your own life." This was followed by the pregnant pause, always a little tricky to interpret on the phone.

Then he said, "Oh. You know about that." This cemented the first connection between us. He knew; I understood his plight. Trading had ruined his life. We reviewed the facts of his family, his church, his finances. I have no need to go into details. Every trader knows his story without me needing to spread out the embarrassing mistakes, always mysteriously foolish when viewed calmly after the fact with the "wisdom" of hindsight.[7] When a trader gets to this point, he or she better hope they have some very forgiving people around them.

My point: There is nothing flippant about my title, even though demoted from the cover to this opening chapter.[8] I admit that it is too private for a book title. But it communicates the traumatic downside of our business. I've known a number

---

[7] There is no business in which hindsight is wiser, easier, and more destructive than trading. A trader with a life-long history of trading problems recently referred to something I had done as "stupid." All you need to do is wait until after the fact and you too will be able to call others stupid.

[8] Truthfully, I'm shocked this title has survived the publisher's process.

of people who have taken this ultimate option. So much so that I've spoken on the topic. My classmates and I have invested a lot of our mental energy over the past decades wondering what path we might have taken that could have prohibited our friend from doing this to himself; we were juniors in high school at the time. You probably already know about Livermore's life and trading style, flamboyant enough to make every trade I ever made look about as exciting as watching paint dry. His widow had already lost her first four husbands to this terrible disease, if we may carelessly call it that. But if suicide is your struggle, stop reading here and go straight to the footnote.[9]

---

[9] If you are in this struggle, I will suppose it is financial. Here are a few things to think about. On second thought, don't think about them; just do them. You'll recover:

1. Read one of the Psalms and take heart. (they are very short, 5 to 10 sentences each)

2. Flex your inclination to procrastination. You've put it off this long; keep putting it off. You can do this tomorrow. You can do this after you've read this book–after you've done this list. There will always be another opportunity to do this. Just put it off.

3. God has a plan for your life. This isn't it.

4. You are doing this to escape regrets. But it will begin your next life with a regret that will never go away.

5. If you are totally convinced that this life is all there is, you won't lose a thing by waiting until tomorrow, or until you're done reading this book.

6. Recall the nicest gift you ever received; that gift was peanuts compared to the gift of your life.

7. Recall the nicest feeling you ever had. You were given life for feelings like that.

8. Contemplate this: The first thing that will happen after your demise will be the showing of a video; it will be the quintessential woulda-coulda-shoulda, showing all the good things that would have happened as a result of you sticking around; you would have enriched the lives of so many. It will be called, *It's an Un-Wonderful Life.*

9. You are in a drawdown. We all have them. I cannot know whether your drawdown is emotional, financial, or spiritual. This is not what matters. What matters is how you come out of it. This is my guarantee–tomorrow your drawdown will look different. If you must do something foolish, wait till tomorrow to do it. Better yet, wait until you have covered chapters four and five. This will help you to understand your situation, how you got into it, how to avoid it in the future.

WHAT? NO TRADE SECRETS? AGAIN!

It was twenty-five years ago that I first published *God in the Pits* with Macmillan. It was never anyone's intention for that book to be a How-To manual for traders. There was not a trade secret to be found in it. Indeed, it could not have been a bigger discouragement to those who wanted to make their fortunes trading the markets. It included a virtual rant against the lottery industry for ripping people off. Macmillan's editors were indignant, saying, "You made your fortune; why do you want to

---

10. Keep reading. Thanks for reading this far. If you continue reading, you will find the answer to your struggle. You think that there is no answer. You are telling yourself right now that this author knows nothing of your struggle. In the last paragraph I guaranteed you that tomorrow will look different. Now I guarantee you that there is an answer to your struggle. Every struggle has its answer.
11. Read the book of Psalms and take heart.
12. Get help. You're getting some impersonal help right now. But you need personal help. For example, the next suggestion.
13. If you are in the market, liquidate. If you've read all the way down to here, your problem must be financial. Get someone to help you liquidate; it's always difficult to liquidate your own losing trades. Tell 'em you're suicidal if you have to. But get someone to get you out. Stop worrying about the market coming back where you always planned that it should go. It will—that is the nature of our industry. The market always goes where you predict that it will—eventually. The only question is: Will you participate in that move? The purpose of this book is to help insure that you will. But for now, if you are still reading, you need to get out of the market. I know what you are thinking: Isn't this just like a writer to tell me to shut the barn door after the horses have left? But the cliché does not apply because if you are still in the market, all the horses are not yet gone (to continue this questionable metaphor). And I'm not writing like a writer; I'm writing like a trader who knows where you are and what you're feeling. Therefore, if you are still in the market, stop reading now, get someone to help you get out, then come back here. Don't do what my friend did—run away and leave someone else to discover your losing position and then have to liquidate it for you. (No one knows how big your losses might be by that time.) That is a legacy no human being wants.
14. Lastly—you will likely need some forgiveness. Forgiveness is far easier to get than you now suppose. Trust me on this; the only place you will find difficulty getting forgiveness is from yourself. (I know whereof I speak, and write.)

8

deny others the same opportunity?" If you catch Macmillan's thinking, you can appreciate the ignorance that is rampant about our industry. The lottery? An opportunity comparable to trading? And the Macmillan editors are the well-educated New Yorkers. Yet they assume that the lottery[10] gives the player the same opportunity I had on the floor of the exchange. If one is in that state of misunderstanding, one needs far more than a trade secret. This is not the last you'll hear on this matter.

WHAT? NO ENTRY SIGNALS? AGAIN!

There was an outcry by a few that my first book offered no buying or selling tips. I'll try once more to explain. No one gives away their market entry points. And no one sells them either. Do you get this? If you do, skip ahead while we take a moment to clarify. Here is a summary of the point, and it will become obvious as we move along.

First, an entry point is only as good as the person who executes it. My son has a brother-in-law who has an office overlooking the Hudson River. One day he was on the phone and surprised the person on the other end of the line when he said, "There is an airplane floating down the Hudson River." Obviously, the other party took it as a joke. The A320 Airbus is an amazing airplane. But I can state categorically that if you or I had been flying that plane, every person on board would now be in their afterlife. It takes more than entry and exit points to make a trader.

Second, the fact that trading systems get sold, proves that we must belabor this point. If a person offers to sell you a sys-

---

[10] I cannot lay off this topic. Henry Fielding is credited with comparing the lottery to a tax on fools. The line is true, for sure. But because Fielding lived three centuries ago, it is impossible to know how much humor he intended. Insulting it is, but funny it is not. Someday African Americans will discover that the lottery targets their communities, is a sophisticate instrument of oppression, and has not improved even one of their schools. When that happens, they will boycott the lottery, bring down a scandalous institution, and lead their communities in a more productive direction.

tem for $3,000, that is because the system is not worth $3,000. Remember? He is a trader; he buys low and sells high. It is probably not worth anything. But if the trader selling it to you cannot use it, you certainly cannot use it either. Trust me in this: He is wrong to sell it to you; and you are foolish to buy it from him. Here is what is even worse: You perpetuate the problem of the marketing of systems by rewarding this questionable behavior.

I've been in this business during five decades, seventies to teens, and I've never heard of a professional trader buying a system of entry rules. Can you spell J. Welles Wilder Jr.? (I admit, I had to look it up.) And I'll also admit to having bought some of these systems—Babcock's for $26. But only for the purpose of stimulating my thinking for new ideas. You are not in the business to take my entry points and piggyback your trading on them. You are here to make your own contribution to our economy. More on this topic as we proceed. For now the short answer: Any entry (or exit) signal that is broadly known is invalid.

THEN WHAT IS THE MOTIVATION?

That brings me to the motivation for this book after all these years. It is not to correct these misunderstandings. That might never be possible. My motivation is to give the "outside" trader an honest opportunity. You see, the computer age has brought the pit closer and closer to the point where one can trade from off the floor and succeed. But the fact that the electronic pit has brought the exchanges to the public does nothing to eradicate the misunderstandings about the financial exchanges, how they work, and how they contribute to the economy. In the old days this problem was easy. We simply told everyone to stay away, and those who didn't listen paid the price. But now, with the markets more accessible, the situation is much more dangerous. There is a legitimate place for trading from off the floor. So I can no longer simply tell you to stay away. Now you can invest, trade, even day-trade. Indeed there is an entire industry out there inviting you to do just that. They make it look easy, and it is. I mean the trading is easy. Buying low and selling high is another story. There are important fundamentals behind this appearance. More on this in chapter two.

THE DEVIL IS IN THE DETAILS

My son called me from college wanting to know the answer to a question from class: What philosopher said, "God is in the details?" I majored in philosophy up through the graduate level and I didn't know. All I'd ever heard was that the devil was in the details, a line that must give Beelzebub great pride and joy.[11] It will resurface in chapter three. And maybe it could apply to our industry as a whole. It is basically a euphemism for, "I've been sold a bill of goods." Mature people don't call others liars. But in our business the slightest piece of deception is so dangerous and so costly that every trader bends far over backward to avoid mentioning any info that might mislead a fellow trader.

When the weatherman predicts a heat wave over the soybean belt, we say, "He's talking his position," and picture him running off the set, calling his broker and taking profits on his long soybean position as his viewers buy to get in on the sure thing. More to come on this sick topic. For now, I'm doing my best to give you an advance of the details that you will surely attribute to the Lord of the Flies when you do encounter them. All these details will not be mentioned by the marketers of trading systems. You might notice that these marketers are not trading themselves; they are making their money facilitating your trading.

My father always told me that the big money in any sure deal is made by serving those about to get rich. For example, he would say, the people who got rich in the gold rush were those who sold picks and shovels.

---

[11] I know there are many of you (even some Christians) who do not believe in the devil. You should be giving thanks for your sheltered lives. If you'd seen what I've seen, you could not imagine how it could come about without the devil—alive and active.

GENIUS IQ NOT REQUIRED

If you suppose you have the IQ for this business, you probably suffer from the smartest-guy-in-the-room syndrome. This will almost certainly guarantee your failure as a trader. I have seen the market go against me with a total disregard for my IQ. So disrespectful. So disgusting. So wrong.

Trading is not about IQ. We like to think it is because those who don't understand our industry fuel that supposition and who are we to deny a thing like that?

I read Edward O. Thorpe's analysis of blackjack in the sixties. If you'd like a case of mental vertigo, go ahead; read one of his books. Obviously, he is a genius and went on to analyze the markets as well. But you don't need to have Thorpe's cranial acumen to be successful in this business. I certainly don't.

Okay—but that's only the good news. Here's the rest. The themes of this book are relatively simple. I'll admit that chapter four will get slightly technical. But only slightly. And you don't have to master the fine details of the formula. You don't even have to know how the formula works. But you must understand the principal behind it. And you must operate on that principle. So here's the bad news: If you cannot understand clearly the themes of this book, you will not be successful in trading. You can take that as a guarantee from me. And to label this as I have, "bad news," is purely a writer's hyperbole. It is, in fact, good news. It will put you on a path to know, before you consume your margin money, if this business is for you.

Well then, if IQ is not the requirement, what is it that makes for a successful trader?

SKILL SET REQUIRED FOR TRADING

This business is personality driven. This is why you have heard it said (over and over) that no one knows what skill set is necessary to make a successful trader. The reason is that there is a wide variety of strategies that can be employed in our industry. This is why everyone laughs when I mention Joseph as a grain trader, the CTA[12] to the Pharaoh. Everyone who knows anything about Joseph lauds him as a spiritual giant while ignoring all the other talents he possessed. Thus it does not occur to them that he might have had a set of skills that they would do well to emulate. We are taught that Joseph's gifts were spiritual, thus not necessarily applicable in the marketplace. However, I remind the theologians that there was no providential dream or angelic visitation that informed Joseph what to buy. He just used his common sense and Pharaoh thought it was brilliant.

This is where personality comes into play. It is my opinion that those whose personalities are inclined to be conservative, go slowly, and panic out of losing trades early, turn out to be the traders who have long and successful careers. They trade with their gut only when their gut says, "I'm going to get sick living with this loss another minute." Then they get out. On account of some personality trait, they keep their trades the right size. In chapters four and five we will put this personality trait into a formula that will keep you on track.

You might also be curious to observe that these traits are not consistent with the alpha male. The desire to be a Wall Street hot shot is precisely where much of the problem begins with many traders. One of the most telling traits in the pits I traded was the almost humble equity with which everyone was treated. The biggest trader in the pit treated the smallest trader in the pit the same as he treated everyone else. Obviously, when he had a hundred to buy, he looked for the big traders. But he often found time to leave the last ten to spread around to the little traders. There was a mysterious lack of classification along success lines. This surprised me. I'd grown up in the middle class with working people. While we weren't ashamed of our financial status, we certainly had no bragging rights. One had to assume, and we all surely did, that successful and wealthy people must have made the same class distinctions we did. Why would they not take some level of pride in their achievement?

---

[12] Commodity Trading Advisor

13

I was wrong, surprised, and confused by this mistake. But the surprise was so pleasant as to make me regret that I hadn't taken this plunge years earlier. There were all different classes of people in the pit and all different levels of wealth. Some spent their afternoons in upstairs lounges gambling with each other, some in the downtown or neighborhood bars, some on the golf course, some playing polo. In the busy markets I figured I had twenty hours to recover, get enough fluid in me for the next trading session, review my mistakes, and get a game plan for the next day.

Now please set aside momentarily my personal stereotypes about the wealthy in order to make an important observation. I doubt that the lack of ego that I observed was accidental. One might guess that the trait plays a critical role. In all my years on the floor, I never heard a trader brag about a trade, never heard a trader brag about the day he had, the month he had, or any other measure of trading success. Not once. If you find that hard to believe, you share my stereotype about the wealthy. But I am going to guess, and it is purely a speculation on my part, that this mysterious trait is at the heart of being a successful trader. When we get to chapter four, we will put some actual numbers to the theorem.

For now let me summarize the concept: The size of your ego is inversely related to your potential to succeed as a trader. The ego is the enemy of the trader. You will be slow to take this seriously. Most of you will think that I missed my calling, that I'm bucking for Dr. Phil's job. Nevertheless, I put the idea on the table early so you can ponder it as you progress. In the old days it took two hands to trade. This left no way to pat yourself on the back at the same time. Today, it takes all your attention. Take your mind off what you are doing for a moment of self-aggrandizement and you will not be happy with the result.

FINANCIAL MARKETS, THE SOCIALLY SANCTIONED CASINO RIGGED IN YOUR FAVOR

Some decades back I ran into a financial advisor named Larry Burkett. He later became well known for creating Christian Financial Concepts. As soon as he learned that I strongly opposed people trading in the futures market, he begged me to come talk to his people. "Mark," he said, "I've been warning them to stay away from the markets for years. Maybe they will pay attention to you." Over the years, Burkett and I became friends. I'll give him the acknowledgement he deserves here, but there will be more to come on him. This claim that the markets are rigged in favor of the pros has some merit. Chapter two will address the problem. Our mandate is to get you on the favorable side of things.

But first we must acquire a more thorough understanding of the industry as a whole. A Washington lobbyist once called me and said, "You'll have to agree not to tell anyone this, but I never really understood your business until I read that story about the purple pencil in that class of second graders."[13] This misunderstanding is widespread, even within the industry. It will help you to have a good understanding of our contribution to commerce.

SAGA OR SUBSTANCE?

Every book has a thesis and the rest is fluff, stuff to fill pages and make it look like a full-fledged book. But in reality it could all have been done in a few lines, saved the reader a fortune in time and effort, and saved the rainforest from destruction for all the paper it took to print the 195 unnecessary pages of a 200-page book. Does this sound like a description of the vast majority of all the term papers we wrote (sorry to include *you* in that)? And I'll add an apology to all my faithful teachers whose time I wasted reading all that fluff; honestly, that apology was heartfelt.

---

[13] I feel free to tell the story on him now because he has passed away and I don't use his name. (*God in the Pits*, chapter one)

In our situation, however, one person's fluff is another's critical guiding principle. So I've tried to provide directions as we go to help you avoid unnecessary material. If you are among the professionals who don't need the introductory material, I already told you to skip to chapter four. This will not be your last invitation to do so. It is as close as you will get to the holy grail. For you beginners, the holy grail has been the joke of the industry. Every pro knows the phrase and uses it for the joke that it is. But chapter four is as close as you will come. The rest is details. If you beginners skip to chapter four, you will seal your fate. You cannot take short cuts in this business.

THE HIGH PRICE OF THE-SMARTEST-GUY-IN-THE-ROOM

Here's a very brief example. A friend and I were doing lunch in one of my favorite dives in our small town. It used to be a small country town, but sprawling suburbia has overtaken us. It's a friendly town and we were joined by a friend of his. Of course my friend knows I'm a professional trader, but his friend had no idea of my occupation. So when the subject turned to our economy and its instability, his friend began to wax eloquent on a number of strategies he had been thinking about for years—how to capitalize on the next market crash, how things are shaping up like '29, how he was going to execute a plan to beat the system and the market if that ever happened again, and more typical jargon, the kind you hear at cocktail parties.

At a number of points in the conversation I tried to make a few observations about some of the big markets I'd traded through. Actually the crash of '87 was even more dramatic in its drop than '29 had been. But it was not possible to get enough of a sentence into the discussion to let this person know that I was a trader. The guy had everything pretty well worked out. He just needed to get his account open and enter his first order.

Finally my friend said, "Mark, we need to tell him who you are." But I shook my head, declining. Listening to such talk is a good exercise. It's humbling—keeps me thinking, *There but for the grace of God go I.* It reminds one of the dangers of going there. But one does fear for that person's family; I hope this book will serve as a warning to those who are seduced down that path. In his case, I doubt he'll ever read this. If he does, I can guarantee that he will miss this section anyway and already be in chapter four. Last I heard he had quit his day job and became a pastor.[14]

HOW MUCH IS TOO MUCH CONFIDENCE

I have not yet met a trader with as much confidence as the person we lunched with that day. Of course it came across as arrogance. But labeling behavior is not our concern. Our concern is to identify the character trait that will assure failure. And one thing is certain–the market does not give you the freedom to have that level of confidence in yourself.

Thus we arrive again at the more critical matters of life. When something as mundane as money can drive one to suicide, as we know it can, one has to consider that we have neglected these weightier issues. Most people, Christians included, place their certitude in their professional skills, and exercise *faith* that the things they believe about God are true.

I do the opposite. And recommend this for traders. Let us search for certitude in what has been called the "weightier matters" of life, and have the less certain "faith" in our actual trades. More on this as we proceed, but the theme must be introduced now to get you thinking about it. If you are an atheist, it won't matter to your trading at all, until it does matter and then it will matter a lot. If you are a theist by faith instead of by evidence and proof, you will find that your faith may not get you through some of our difficult times.

---

[14] This only sounds like a joke. But it is true. Please use discretion, prayer, and wisdom in evaluating what pastors to avoid.

THE HIGH PRICE OF IGNORANCE

I credit my friend, the late Larry Burkett, with this story about an investor who put a small fortune down on a thoroughbred, saying to himself, "All you have to do is keep your pet alive, and certainly happy, and you can collect stud fees for twenty years." Hey, what could go wrong? Well, in the case of the thoroughbred, it turned out to be a gelding. I can still see Larry laughing while asking, "Did you take a look under there?" The punch line to this story is that it's not a joke. Our industry is most fitting to such stories and they need no exaggerating.

If you are successful in this business, you will be approached by traders looking for someone to capitalize their trading ideas. It will take you a while to learn that this is a bad idea. I learned this the hard way. I capitalized a trading analyst who came highly recommended. And his analysis of the market was outstanding. And what's more, we were in a bull market. It doesn't take a genius to make money in a bull market.

Here's a hot tip for you, straight from the floor: *Never confuse brilliance with a bull market.* So after a day or two of trading, with his account up by about 30 percent, I suggested that he was overtrading. He agreed and began trading smaller. A week later, I noticed that I had not seen him for a few days. In the middle of one of the wildest markets in memory, one has no time or energy to oversee another trader's activity. He had simply disappeared and left no info as to where he was or what he was doing. But of course I knew who would be responsible for his trades. And he left open positions, obviously short, which ate up all his profits, all the capital I had assigned to him, and a whole lot more. By the way–remember that warning? "You can lose more than you have." Do not make the mistake of thinking that it is overstated legalese.

There's more to this story, as there always is. But for now let this chapter close with the first lesson: Character matters. Every professional trader knows that you don't believe that; we hold that opinion because we think that all you want is entry and exit points. But there is so much more to trading than entries, exists, and even accurate analysis. This particular trader-wannabe continued and made quite a name for himself in the industry, wrote analytical articles for Futures Magazine, even published a book, and progressed from failure to failure as a trader. During this same period of time, many a trader partnered with me or CRT and had successful careers. None of these traders had that analyst's ability to exude confidence, articulate strategies, and analyze the markets. If you read his analysis or talked to him today, you would be impressed and happy to trade his recommendations with great confidence. Professional traders, reading those last two sentences will recognize the trap right away. It is the classic case of too much confidence.

It will be the purpose of this book to demonstrate why that analyst failed. Of one thing I am certain—it had nothing to do with his market insight; his market analysis was great. If you asked him for an opinion on the market and then asked me for a second opinion, I can assure you that his opinion will be worth far more than mine. He was better than I at such analysis. To this day he is a respected market analyst and writer. It's his trading, and his character, that was the problem.

FYX (FOR YOU CHRISTIANS)

It is altogether fitting in this business that we Christians should begin in Torah. I think we can assume that the pros have skipped on ahead, the non-believers are gone, and we still have some details to cover. You don't *have* to be a believer to stick around here. I can't keep you away. If you'd like to invade the sort of thinking that goes on inside the minds of people who are tempted to be (as we say), "so heavenly minded we are of no earthy use," you are welcome to read this stuff. But I'm warning you that it won't serve you very well. You won't need it for your trading. It will remind you of the fluff, the extra 95 percent to fill the book. It is not. It's important to those of us who are still confused about a variety of issues often referred to as unrighteous mammon.[15]

Now about that Torah. Let us begin with the first words ever to come from the mouth of God. Look at Genesis 1:28. There are four directives here, commands virtually.

1. Be fruitful
2. Multiply
3. Fill the earth
4. Subdue it.

It's that first one that is most ignored. You cannot meet this spiritual requirement if you buy high and sell low. I call it spiritual because it came from God. You might call it generous, at least for the person you trade with. But it is not productive. And you are called to be productive; that means you must turn a

---

[15] I will deal with that famously abused line about money being the root of all evil, but not in the FYX section. I've heard pastors twist the scripture to meet their needs. But we don't need professional theologians to twist it for us. It is in the nature of our world for scripture to get twisted. And please observe that point. You need not be a Greek scholar to see it. This is critical, does not belong in the FYX section, and will come up repeatedly. For now—money is not the root of all evil. False theology is more effective outside the church than inside. Go to this website and you can check up on the Greek scholars: http://biblehub.com/interlinear/1_timothy/6-10.htm In this case I have sent you directly to the scripture reference that is so often abused. You can see it in Greek even though it is just as clear in English.

profit. Those whose spiritual maturity surpasses yours and mine have invited us to become the servants of humanity, i.e., do God's work by serving others. Who can complain about that? But most of the spiritually mature people who do that service have forgotten that they can only eat and do that work if they are supported by someone who is being productive. Let us refrain from judging them for this oversight. But let us remember, based on this directive from God, that those of us who buy low and sell high are not engaged in unrighteous, secular work. God told us to do it.

We have been convinced by our spiritual superiors that God's work is done in the church and by those in spiritual authority. It has been an easy mistake for them to make because they have heard it from all their instructors beginning the first day they decided to go into God's work. But they are making a natural and an honest mistake as we will show in these FYX sections.

Renowned Christian publisher, Moody Press, once had an editor who liked my writing and attempted to get something of mine published. If you can picture the typical author angst at this point, I can spare you my heart-rending stories. At the end of the aforementioned stories, which I have spared you, one of their editors had a moment of candor in which he said, "Mark, truthfully, we just don't like your style." It took me about a year, maybe two, to persuade myself that this was actually a compliment. I started my first book with the now infamous "Sex-in-the-elevator" story. What did I expect from a publisher with a motto, "A name you can trust?"

So I confess: I don't fit the Christian writer mold. If you want a name you can trust, get a Moody book. They are outstanding and trustworthy in the extreme. But if you want to know how to buy low, sell high, and trade with people who do things in the elevator, stick with me. Those people have the same need to be loved that we have.

CHAPTER TWO

IS THE PLAYING FIELD LEVEL YET?

Stephen King can write about rats going down people's throats, elicit the horror, and make a fortune. This is a pipe dream for the rest of us writers. Publishers make money; writers write. But that doesn't mean I don't have the horror stories. And the rats in my stories will devour your 401k, your life savings, even your house. After one brief talk on this topic, I was approached by a young woman. She was dressed and made up to look as if she had just stepped off a photo shoot for the cover of Vogue. I'd never seen anything like her up close. But when I looked into her eyes I saw panic. Her husband had been trading, had just disappeared, and what could she do now? Her eyes told me that she had lost everything. She had a small child on each hand.

Stephen King makes up the horror and collects the money. In our business, we create the horror and the money flows in the other direction.

In the good ol' days I argued strongly against outsiders speculating in our business. The playing field was not level—not even close. For example, a struggling trader once called me for some advice. So I asked him what he was paying in commissions. He said, "About ten dollars a round turn." That basically means that he paid five to buy and five to sell. And he did this for every contract. So if he traded a ten lot, it cost him a hundred dollars. I told him that if he took all the trades I'd made in my career and charged them at his rate, I would have gone broke a long time ago.

In those days, the difference between a successful career and bankruptcy was fairly easy to identify; the cost of doing business made it totally prohibitive for anyone from outside the industry. Naturally, if one came to the floor of the exchange, pushed, shoved, and yelled their head off with the rest of us, you would have the same low cost of transactions that we had. And you would find plenty of traders, myself included, who would give you more advice than you could have used to help you get your career off the ground.

But trading from off the floor? Forget it. It was not a level playing field. The trader I mentioned was *only* paying $10 a round turn. In prior years $100 a round turn was not out of the ordinary. Does that answer the question why so many lost money trading commodities? Remember Duke and Duke in "Trading Places?" They summed it up when they said, "We make money no matter what happens to the client."

There was, in the pit, a talented trader who broke his arm one summer playing softball. Here in Chicago we play 16-inch ball exclusively, no gloves, and serious stuff.[16] So he went upstairs and traded from the office until he got his cast off. I won't mention his name for lack of permission, but I doubt he would mind if I did. And everyone who knows him will remember this

---

[16] They will soak a bat in the swimming pool all winter, then shellac it and keep it standing so the moisture stays in the barrel. In the first two innings, the ball, always new, is very hard. The pitcher must have cat-like reflexes. One year I was playing left field for the Cook County Correctional Officers team and we came up against one of the those very serious Chicago PD precincts. Someone came to the plate whom the jail warden knew. He came running down the left field line yelling at me to back up. I backed up a ridiculous distance only because it was the warden. From the moment the ball left the bat I knew I was in trouble, even though I was already almost as deep as if I'd been playing baseball. I did get a hand on it. When I picked it up, I was at second base in the girls' field at the other end of the park.

story. He almost went broke that summer, trading from off the floor, waiting to get the cast off his arm. We could guess that he might have been paying about $3 a round turn.

That was then. This is now. Today modern technology has brought the pit to us in ways that make it much more cost effective to trade from off the floor, get transaction cost low enough, and be able to get in and out with a profit margin left over. The same rules of open outcry apply and are coded into trading platforms in a way that make the execution of trades far more efficient than ever before. As a trader, soon to be considered an antique, I personally have hated to see the open outcry of the pit pass away. There was something about seeing and hearing prices move that forced all transactions out into the open.

It is true that a good computer program can do this even better. But I'm not a computer whiz so I often wonder who is in control of the code. I recognize a good trade when one gets executed on my behalf. And so far, the computerized pit has proven itself. While that is not universally true, it only takes one good pit to prove it can be done. And it surely has been done. The point is that I no longer have the reason I once had to discourage trading from off the floor. I trade from off the floor myself.

Peter Brandt, trading guru for many decades, has kindly agreed to read the early manuscript and share his thoughts. But he hastened to add, "Beware, I am no fan of day-trading. I think it is a trap for new traders looking to get rich."

And you readers beware too. I agree with Brandt. The fact that the playing field is now level will not insure your profitability. It will only entice you to continue to invest. This could, in fact, make matters worse. I wrote of this extensively in my first book, and have spoken of it at length. Earlier I mentioned Macmillan's frustration; they thought I was trying to keep everyone away from my pot at the end of the rainbow. That is, of course, not true, as this book is intended to show.

So the good news is that the computer age has brought the pit to us and has leveled the field to the point where it is safe to trade. Now that we are done with the good news, here comes the bad. There is no level playing field anywhere. There will always be dishonest people who make life difficult for all of us who try to shoot straight. Fred Schwed's book of a century ago said it all with the title, "Where are the Customer's Yachts?" It's a sad state of affairs.

I have been very complimentary of the people with whom I traded in the pits and complimentary of the integrity of the Chicago Board of Trade. I told a story about some of the dignitaries at the CBT who didn't give my brother and me the greatest respect when we first walked in wearing cheap, poorly fitting suits. But that story has nothing to do with the CBT's goal of fair trading. In fact, given how we looked, we probably got more respect than we deserved. That was an attention-getting, human-interest story. But hey—that's life. The reader must take confidence in this: In our business, no one cares if your suit doesn't show well, or any of the rest of the long list of things that keep you out of the "right" crowd. Your order goes into the computer system like everyone else's.[17]

All the advances of the computerized pit notwithstanding, the playing field is still not level; never has been; never will be. However, it is now level enough for you to play on it. But this does not mean that everyone is looking out for you. There's still a lot to learn.

Example: I had an account at E*TRADE where the fees were low enough that if I entered a large trade, my per-share cost was tolerable. I entered an order on a Friday morning. An hour later I cancelled the order and got confirmation of my cancel. I think it was for 10,000 shares. When I looked at my account on Wednesday morning, I noticed that I had a larger position than I expected. So I examined Tuesday's trades and found that a buy of 10,000 shares had been entered into my account after Tuesday's close. But it was at a price that was out

---

[17] Not universally true, as the brilliant author, Michael Lewis, has shown. But those who have invested millions to short circuit the trading system will find themselves out of business eventually.

of Tuesday's range. In fact, it was entered as an "As of," order, meaning that it was "as of" Friday's trading range. Sure enough, this was the order that had been cancelled on Friday. Obviously, the market had moved and some local market-maker had the ability to fill the order way after the fact. I lost thousands getting out of that trade. When your profit margin is about $100, a trader does his best to keep his losses in the hundred-dollar range as well. It takes a lot of wins to overcome a theft of that size.

That trade is an example of an unlevel playing field that no amount of great trading can overcome. I have not entered a trade at E-Trade since that incident. This book cannot tell you how to protect yourself from that sort of incident. It can only warn you that there are still places you cannot trade and survive.

While I'm proud of an industry that has achieved a modicum of a level playing field, this does not mean that the folks are looking out for you. There remains a great body of information that must be acquired, and a learning curve.

The vast network about which Fred Schwed wrote is still in place. While the following story is a slight generalization, here's how it works. Let us suppose you have an order to sell 10,000 shares of XYZ stock. And your broker places that order, let's say at $15 a share. This is a fair price because in this hypothetical market that I have made up, there are buyers trying to buy it at 14 and 15/16. When the broker sells your 10,000 shares at $15, he immediately begins to bid 14 and 15/16 to buy the 10,000 back. If he can get it bought back, both the buy and the sell go into his account. And his official report to you is that you are still working to sell your XYZ stock at $15.

I was told that a broker has two hours to decide in which account to place an executed order. When my associate and I learned about this strange situation, we both looked at each other and said, "How can anyone resist the temptation to do this?" In the commodities market where I spent my career, every order had an account before it went into the market.

Changing the account on an order after it was filled was sure to get you kicked off the exchange, if not put in jail.

When your broker tells you that he was unable to fill your order, he is telling you a legal lie. He may have filled your order ten times, all liquidated profitably and placed in his account. And he calls this a level playing field. (So does his wife, and the kids at their private school.) To answer Fred Schwed's question, this is why *there are no* customer yachts. The good trades go into the broker's account, and you will only sell your XYZ stock when the market goes 15 bid. As we say in this business, "You get filled exactly when you don't want it."

You should have already noticed that I have great respect for our industry, for the service it provides, and for the excellence with which it does it. In the wake of 9/11, an attack specifically aimed at our industry, we reopened trading seven days later. Every respectable trader I've ever known is deeply shamed by the "hypothetical" theft about which I just wrote. We're not in business to steal from anyone. We're not in business to even take unfair advantage of anyone. Are the "dishonest"[18] brokers just described in my story in the minority? Honestly, I do not know. But you must be able to avoid them.

One year I found myself doing some business solely for a few friends and relatives. It soon began to require quite a bit of stock trades. So I offered this business to a number of high-level account managers. My best estimate was that it was about $100,000 in commission business per year. This was obviously of interest to them. All I asked was that they guarantee me the integrity of my orders. They knew that I meant that I didn't want my orders "leaned on." My friends, Sunday morning hymn singers all, had enough integrity to tell me that they could not give me that guarantee. The point: Those who would love to create a level playing field are powerless to do so.

---

[18] "Dishonest," is in quotes because this is legal. You could not convince them of that such behavior is dishonest. I have tried. If they won't listen to me, they won't listen to you.

So you must know what it means to have your order leaned on. There are some houses who make all their money this way. They would take your orders and fill them for free. The problem is that this would make it obvious that they were leaning on their customer's orders. This is a common practice.

Okay, I'm a professional so I can tell when I'm being taken advantage of unfairly. It's not too difficult for me to identify an honest broker. In fact, I formed a partnership with two of them, both wonderful Christian professionals. One day their firm was working an order for me at a price, just like the story above; my recollection was that the price was 12. When I noticed that the market had traded at 12 1/16 a lot of times, I asked for a fill.[19] My friend, the head broker, informed me that our partner was not able to fill the order because he was trying to get a better price for me. I counted the times it had traded at 12 1/16. It had traded there 84 times.

So I told my friend that the only fair thing was for them to give me my fill at 12. The market was now at 11 1/2. He said he would check with his associate brokers to see if that was fair. They all agreed that he had no obligation to give me a fill.

Now you should understand that the way business is done in the commodity world, when the market trades at *any* price above 12, every broker with an order to sell at 12 is obligated to give his customer a fill. It would never occur to a broker to be free of that obligation. In fact, the client would never have to ask for the fill. That trade would be made automatically by the broker no matter how much money it cost the broker to make the client whole. Such is not the case in stocks.

So I was a little surprised by their lack of commitment to my order. But they were my partners and friends and they said they were backing off in an attempt to get me a better price. So they refused to give me the fill at 12.

Sometime later my broker called to give me evidence of their trading skill on my behalf. He was offering proof that they

---

[19] If you are a beginner, "fill" is a verb that means "to execute" an order. Here it is in the noun form, i.e., an order that has been executed in the market.

were seeking to fill my order at a higher price. He said, "Our partner, one of the best order fillers in this business, has been waiting to get you a better fill. And he did. You wanted to sell at 12 and he sold it higher." This is a typical broker bragging item. And it has its place. There certainly are times that a broker fills an order very well. Usually a great fill will be obvious. But if it's not, no one minds a broker stating that he got a great fill on an order, a simple matter of professional pride. Nothing is nicer in this business than a great fill. Brokers are well paid, and a good fill proves that they earn it. So this is what my friend was calling to tell me. The message: See Mark, I told you so. Your broker is serving your interest.

When I traded on the floor, the quality of every fill was obvious. But now, trading off the floor, a good fill is not at all obvious. So it is altogether fitting for a broker, proud of a job well done, to call and make something of it.

While my broker was telling me how well they had done by backing off and getting me a better price, I put the price chart for that stock up on my computer. Here's what it looked like:

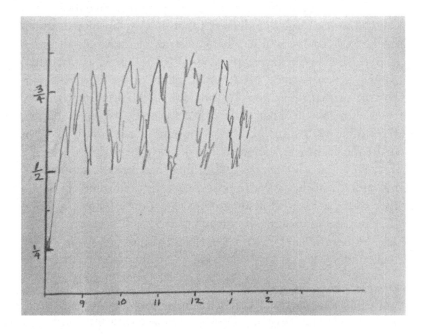

We need to have a close look at this chart because it is critical for you to be able to identify a good fill. You should be able to see that value on this chart is just over 5/8. This day would be a day-trader's dream; sell at 3/4 and take profits at 5/8 or even 9/16. So any purchase below 5/8 would give a broker bragging rights. A buy at 9/16 would be sensational and a buy at 1/2 would be cause for celebration and thanksgiving. On the sell side, anything above 5/8 is okay, above 11/16 is great, and above 3/4 is a dream fill. Just for clarity, the trade at 1/4 is an aberrant, a left-over trade from the previous day. Someone had a sell in at 1/4 and obviously it got picked up easily on the open when value was clearly at 1/2. Usually these trades have little if any volume.

Okay, you have the picture. So where do you suppose my broker, friend, partner had executed my order, the one he was now calling me to brag about, the one that was displaying how talented he was at getting me the best fills available? Place your guesses now please, before proceeding to the next paragraph.

While you are getting ready for this, I will admit that I'm feeling a little adrenaline going as I recall that my order was filled at 1/4. If it had only been a buy order, there would be plenty of bragging rights to be had. But it was a sell order. Clearly word had gotten out overnight that the stock was due for a rally. The only trade below 1/2 was my trade, on the opening at 12 1/4. In fact, my friend-partner-broker had been offering my trade at 12 when the market opened at 12 1/2. That was why I got the "better" fill at 12 1/4. And of course, this is why that particular trade never went into my friend-partner-broker's account. *It was no good.* Who wants to sell something at 12 1/4 when the market is trading at 12 5/8? But my broker thinks that I wanted to sell it at 12 and I sold it at 12 1/4. I never did find out how many times he sold it there. Discovering that would require a major investigation. The only way I could get filled was when value changed to 12 5/8. And even then I sold it for 3/8 less than what it was worth. The only bragging done on this day was by the guy who bought my 10,000 shares at a quarter and pocketed a quick $2,500. Very quick.

Hint: If you are having any trouble grasping the concept behind this story, back up and review until you do. You can invest in Apple or Walmart, hold them for five years and make good money without getting great fills on your buy and sell orders. You cannot day-trade like that. You cannot. All the wisdom in all the trading books will not do anything for you if you cannot tell the difference between a good and a bad fill.

I said to my friend, "Why are you calling me and lying like this? You know that I'm a professional. I can tell if the broker backed off or if he was picked off and made to look like a trading fool." He insisted that I got a better price than I had originally wanted. I sold the stock at 12 1/4 when my order was to sell it at 12.

You can suppose that I should have made a copy of that chart and taken legal action. But the fact is that they had done nothing wrong. In the stock market, it is perfectly legal. *You* know it's immoral. *I* know it's dishonest. Every *client* knows it's theft. But why are we complaining; I got a better fill.

If you are having difficulty understanding that the story I just told is theft, you will not be able to be a trader. You can do investing, but try to limit yourself to no more than one trade per month.

Most of the people I spent my career trading with are deeply ashamed of the story I just told. We are not in this business to rip people off. This habit is called, "leaning on your orders." If the trade is a good one, meaning if it can be liquidated at a profit, it goes into the broker's account. If it is a bad one, it goes to the client.[20]

When this broker and I had a falling out, he suggested that we had a personality conflict. You may recall from the previous chapter the comment that trading is often personality driven.

---

[20] Trust me in this: You can make a lot more money stealing than you can trading. It's easier, quicker, and more reliable.

So maybe it is my personality. There is something about ripping people off that leaves me unsatisfied.

Remember now, your job is to buy low and sell high. That means that you must buy when you perceive that true value is higher than the market thinks it is. And sell when the reverse is the case. But in the story I have laid out for you, I did just the opposite. I failed to sell when I should have and could have. And I did sell when I should not have. As we say in the business, you got it exactly when you didn't want it.

You must be able to identify a good fill. You know that the fill I got from E-trade is the poster child for bad fills. However, the really bad ones are the ones you don't notice. The only way I noticed that "better" fill was because my friend called to brag about it. These fills will slip right on by, you give up a bit of your profit margin, and you keep on trading using brokers who give you bad fills.

When I ran a fund, my partner and I had personal experience in every pit we traded. We knew who the good brokers were and we secured the guarantee from every clearing broker that all our trades would go to the specific brokers we named. One day we got a fill in the British Pound that I didn't like. I didn't know that broker personally, but my partner did. And I knew that no respectable broker would give a fill like this one. (I cannot now recall the specifics.) So I called the floor and told them that I did not want to complain about a specific trade; there's is no way to get any details on any single trade after the fact. But I said, "Just tell me who filled that order." Sure enough, it was not the broker they had agreed would handle all our orders. They could not figure out how I had selected from all the orders that day, the one trade they had messed up.

Three things are certain in life. You know the first two; the third is bad fills. And the only way to limit them is to be able to recognize them when they come. If you day-trade, the quality of your fills will make a huge difference in your track record. It will likely prove to be the difference between success and failure. If you are an investor, holding Apple and adding more stock to your position as the years prove it to be a good trade, your fills won't matter much. But if you want to be a day-trader, as your trading volume increases, the importance of your fills increases. In the old days of notoriously terrible fills, enormous commissions (remember $100 a round turn), and the trend-is-your-friend philosophy, there was only one choice: Make a trade and pray for a trend to develop. You did not have the ability to get in, cut your loss, get in again, cut your loss, and get in again. That was a sure-fire losing strategy simply because of the expense. But now that your transaction costs are under control, you must look at your cost of execution. The cost of execution is much more difficult to identify, and usually impossible to measure. But you cannot day-trade without some handle on this cost.

If you are not understanding this principal, there is no need for you to progress on to chapter four. It will merely mislead you into thinking you are ready to trade when you are not. No amount of market wisdom will offset bad execution. And every broker worth his salt will guarantee you excellent execution. Please understand: All system research is hypothetical until you begin to actually execute the trades. This is why no professional trader will take paper trading seriously. Someone made this observation: Paper-trading is to real trading as shadow boxing is to the real thing. I've never boxed and I can still capture the power of this analogy, which is spot on.

In the case I have mentioned, I have no idea how often our firm (my partners and friends) had sold the market at 12 or 12 1/16 and bought it back at 11 15/16 or 12. But I counted eighty-four times that it traded above my price. So it would be reasonable to assume that they might have been able to trade it at my price as many as 500 times. We'll never know for sure, but this is certainly possible. And it is further reasonable to guess that the vast majority of these trades were taken off at a profit, i.e., 11 15/16. Again, we are guessing; many may have been scratched at 12. But we may be certain that they had made a good profit trading between 12 1/16 and 11 15/16. If this seems like a minute profit margin, you are a novice; proceed with the utmost caution.

Now here is the important point: Their position size is, of course, the factor which determines the profit in these single-tic trades. And their position size is identical to the size of my order. It may have been 20,000 shares in this case, making each trade worth 20,000 tics–$1,250. Remember I said that I counted 84 trades at 12 1/16, thus making it impossible to guess how many they might have been able to make at the $12 mark, but 100 or more would be easily possible. In fact, the eighty-four trades only represented a half of one day. And this order stayed in the market for over two weeks. Naturally, not every sale they made would be for 20,000 shares. If they sold 10,000 at 12 they would immediately begin bidding for 10,000 shares at 11 15/16 while offering the rest (10,000 shares) at 12.

In short, they can dominate the market and all the trades go into their account. If they could do it only 100 times, the profit is $125,000. And that is just the profit achieved by leaning on *my* order. This is how brokers very quickly become (in their own minds) the smartest people in the room.

Do me a favor: Don't ever scoff at a 1/16 profit margin (more often 1/32 or even 1/64). If you are an investor, this may not be a big deal to you. But this is a book about trading. If you are a trader, your profit per trade will, of necessity, be much smaller. If you lose 1/16 on your fill, it will very likely make all the difference. It might not seem like a lot to you, but your wife and family will know the difference. That profit margin, no matter how small, is the bread and butter of wealth creation. In this case, all the profit was stolen. But you could never convince those brokers (my friends and partners, remember?) of that. One man's "theft" is another man's "productivity." We can pray that the day will come when some regulatory body will stop this practice (widespread as it is), but don't hold your breath.

Your reaction to the last paragraph should be, "Well, duh." If the duh factor does not come immediately to your mind, you do not have the instincts to be a trader. Stick with investing.[21]

This is exactly what happened to me, and I'm a professional. And the orders were executed by my friends and partners. Are you getting the picture? You don't have a chance.

So now you have the good, the bad, and the ugly news about the playing field. And you still want to trade? At least you now know that the Peter Brandts of the trading world are keeping you away for your own good. But if you are a glutton for this kind of punishment, and you've said "duh" a bunch over the past ten pages, then chapter three awaits. No doubt we are thinning the ranks of readers from the crowd because we have a saying in our business, one of the best in the business: The crowd is always wrong.

I love that line. You will learn to love that line. If not, we will add one more reason for you to avoid the world of trading.

---

[21] If you don't know the difference between trading and investing, get help. Here's a general rule: If you make less than one trade a week, you are an investor. If you make more than ten trades a week, you are a trader. If you are in between one and ten, you are double-minded; get help. The point is: If you're going to be in the deep end of the pool, stop hanging onto the side.

FYX

You may begin with Psalm 15:4 and go from there. You'll be hard pressed to find a page of holy writ that does not speak of integrity. Having theology that is correct is a high priority to us Christians; but the bible is about living a life of integrity.

There are many Christians who think adopting our faith is in itself an act of integrity. You should now be laughing. Because this is some sort of theological joke perpetrated on the elect by you know who, the enemy of every soul. If this joke does not convince you unbelievers in the existence of a devil, nothing else will. (You should now be in the next chapter anyway.)

I pray you are not among those who think that being a Christian is the ultimate act of integrity. When Christians make this mistake, their faith actually inoculates them from the hard work that integrity demands.

There may be a scripture verse on every page of holy writ that speaks to this foolishness. I will not spoon feed them to you; go find them on your own. Our faith does not guarantee us character. It still must be developed. I'm trying to get back into Proverbs to work on my own shortcomings.

The partner-friend in my story was a fine upstanding Christian, still a leader in his church and among his Christian friends. Your Christian faith will not deliver you the character you need free of charge. Character is developed a little like an athlete, one exercise at a time. And the problem is that you will never get any credit for it. You know how we Christians like to get credit for every act of righteousness. But integrity is a private matter. What credit do you get for doing the right thing when everyone is watching? This explains why it is rare, even in Christian circles, especially in Christian circles.

My father had it. And he did his dead-level best to pass it on to me, an effort I never appreciated during his lifetime.[22]

---

[22] cf. *God in the Pits* for the details on that compliment. An interviewer once said to me, "You know who the real hero of this book is, don't you?" When I paused, he answered, "Your father." One day I was filling my car with gas at the pump on the grounds of the ministry where he worked. (He only did a few

But character is not something that you pass on or hand out. It's born in a crucible of stress and pain. My Christian broker-friend seemed to know that he needed more integrity. He even asked me to help him develop it. (Okay–for you non-believers who have snuck in here, without permission, this is what many of us Christians do for each other to help us see our blind spots. We call it giving "accountability.") This meant that he possessed the typical Christian confusion, i.e., how does the golden rule fit with the dog-eat-dog rules of engagement. But the transition to integrity is not easy and is almost always accompanied by great fear of reduction of income.

So I did what he asked; I confronted him seriously about his dishonesty. I said, "I'm giving you accountability. I'm telling you exactly what you need to do to be an honest broker." I generally gave him the sort of information summarized here.

The fact that your pastor doesn't know what you're doing gives you no excuse for giving anyone a fill like the one here described. James speaks specifically to this situation when he asks, "What about the details of your business dealings?"[23] Business is business? Yes. You have to make a profit? Sure. But there is no excuse for ripping people off. And if you think you can do it and avoid meeting a God who is very angry, you are sadly mistaken. Non-believers do not have this problem. They don't know any better. But you do. We are called to live by the golden rule. How is it possible to live by the golden rule and brag about a sale at 1/4 when value is 5/8? It is an act of

---

years of Christian ministry work and that was after I left home.) All the staff filled up their cars there because the gas was so much cheaper. Being young and naive, I asked about it and he explained that as a tax-free ministry, the gas was tax-free as well. I gave him an inquisitive look and he said, "This is what Sun Myung Moon went to jail for." I gave him another quizzical look and he said, "I fill up my car at the gas station in town." The level of integrity exemplified inside most Christian sub-cultures would not be sufficient to do business at the CBOT (he said, hanging his head in shame). You may consider this an insult to the Christian community or a compliment to the CBOT. Take your pick. But until you have spent as much time as I have in both communities, you do not have the option to dispute that opinion.

[23] James 5:4, or Jeremiah 22:13

pure hypocrisy to which Christians have become accustomed, primarily because the pastor is totally unaware of what is going on and the layman does not know how the scripture applies.

Actually there was no need to confront this Christian broker about my bad fill; he had done much worse. A shortage of integrity *always* expands. He had cheated a widow out of her life savings. I told him that if he didn't give the widow her money back, he would meet a God who would make my anger look like child's play; and my finger was in his face. I sure hope the non-believers have taken my advice and are over in chapter three. This is no endorsement for the faith—one of the few spiritual points on which I anticipate no argument from the theologians.[24]

Let us relax, remember that hypocrisy will be with us to the end, and reduce the blood pressure slightly. Then focus on our problem; buy low, sell high, and work the golden rule in there somehow. Remember our hero, Joseph? I don't mind when Christians laugh at my suggestion that he was a grain speculator. They are not professional traders. They have no idea what is happening in our industry. So they think I'm joking when I speak about Joseph buying 20 percent of the crop every year. Nonsense. There's no comedy here. And it is safe to assume that he didn't give the farmers the kind of trade I got. No; in fact, he kept the farmers in business with his seven-year buying program. Without Joseph buying, the farmers could never have made a profit in years three through seven. Nothing kills the grain industry like bumper crops in every field. The price drops below production cost almost immediately. Joseph's buying program kept them in production.

And in the end, years eight through fourteen, he made a fortune for the Pharaoh. The rich got richer. The poor survived.

---

[24] I was conversing with my broker one day about my faith and his lack of it. His father had had set an example of faith for him and had recently passed away. So he said to me, "If I become a Christian will I end up like ____?" and he filled in that blank with the name of a broker we both knew very well, known for his Christian faith and his highly questionable trading practices. He'd lost his previous job due to his lack of integrity. So I said, "If you do, I'll fire you as my broker."

Joseph's weather report was divinely inspired. His trading strategy was not. Do not confuse these two. Do not attempt to spiritualize your trading decisions. Whenever you find yourself praying about the market, take it as a sign from the Lord to do exactly what he told that rich young ruler to do—liquidate.

Lest anyone be confused, Joseph is not where the Jewish people got their reputation for financial wizardry. My Jewish friends who may have taken the liberty to sneak into this section—you ought to have been taught by Bernie Madoff all you need to know about the foolishness of over spiritualizing your financial decisions. To all of you I say, "If you have not said to yourself, 'Well, duh,' about half a dozen times while reading this chapter, YOU CANNOT TRADE." If you insist on continuing through this book, you will soon conclude that I have taken a very negative approach. True. Starting with the prevention of suicide, it is my goal to gain control over the negative side of our industry. That means controlling losses. If it is true of you that you cannot trade, I can make you a fortune by keeping you out of our business.

Do not think for a minute that I am discouraging you from becoming a capitalist. That's different. I would that you all should be as I am, a capitalist. Every one of us invests. And we Christians will be held accountable for every investment. Jesus knew a lot about wealth, poverty, and investing. Check out his parables.[25] I invest in orphans. The return is difficult to measure. But if we could assess the ROI,[26] it would be significant; and that is no reference to heaven. My call to capitalism does not mean you should trade. So if you still have the fire in the belly for the pain of this business, and you've said "duh" a bunch over the past ten pages, let us continue on to, "The crowd is always wrong." I love this line. If you do not love this line when you finish chapter three, you cannot trade.

---

[25] And you must look at them with a modicum of originality. E.g. the prodigal; great financial themes here, consistently overlooked.
[26] return on investment

THE CROWD IS ALWAYS WRONG

Some years back I took my family on a vacation to the Middle East. We loved the market in the old city of Jerusalem where you bargain your heart out and the merchants bargain back with far greater talent. I was introducing my kids to the whole game of buying low, almost a contact sport in the Moslem Quarter. The shops are crowded, the streets only wide enough for foot traffic, and very little light comes in through the narrow passageways. Then there is the aroma—bread baking, fresh wool being cleaned and woven, a little open sewage here and there, everything needed to transport one to another time and place.

One afternoon something happened. It may have been standard rush hour. But there were too many people for the space and every person wanted out of that section of the city, and fast. Within about thirty seconds the place turned into a stampeding mob. The cobblestones made for a horrible surface. It became an instant athletic challenge to keep from going down. Our eldest son, Dan, at 230 pounds and all-area center, grabbed his six-year-old sister; I grabbed her twin. Nancy grabbed our ten-year-old son, and Joey, at eleven was on his own. Thankfully, we kept our feet under us and moved in precision with that crowd. Even Dan was not about to stand up against it.

I still recommend the strategy. When you find yourself in a mob, concentrate on one thing alone–keep your feet under you. The crowd will take care of the rest.

Remember this picture and make sure that you do not apply it to your trading. If you find yourself trading with the crowd, do not be afraid to be the first to get off the bandwagon. You do not want to profit from the end of the move. You want to be out before the final upswing. Because remember: *The crowd is always wrong.* And this advice is coming from a trader who once rode a trend for almost four years.[27]

It's a safe assumption that professional traders have already skipped this chapter. No concept will separate the pro from the novice faster than this one. Every pro knows it and trades by it. The rest of you are confused at what this line could mean and why it is so important to us. If you are to become a trader, you will need a thorough understanding of this quip.

Here's a quick example: Some of you are saying, "I'm in chapter three and this guy has still not given me so much as one entry point. Not one! Will he ever?"

And the answer is, "No." Every professional trader fully understands why. And the reason you don't understand why is because this lesson about the crowd is not second nature to you—yet. The pros may have dumped the book upon seeing this chapter, assuming the entire book too remedial. The only reason a pro might still be reading this chapter is to see if I can explain the point—to the crowd. You see the problem? It is not easy to tell a crowd that they are always wrong. But it is true.

Let us suppose that I give in to the pressure and give you an entry point. Here it is: Monday morning is a good buying

---

[27] This would probably be nothing out of the ordinary for Richard (The-trend-is-your-friend) Dennis and his turtles. But for a trader like me, who has one goal–get rid of it ASAP–a four-year run is an anomaly. Merrill Oster looked up, trying to think of a chart that would reflect that and said, "I hope you came out alright on that."

day. All those account executives are getting their buying done, which causes a Monday morning rally. Not always, but most of the time. So I give you this entry point. I tell you to buy the open on Monday morning, put in a short stop[28], and take your profit before the account execs go to lunch at noon.

Remember our theme: The crowd is always wrong. And now the crowd, i.e., everyone reading this book, is using my entry point. They all have their buy orders in for Monday's open. Do you see that you have completely ignored this first lesson of trading? If the crowd is doing it, it is wrong. That is the lesson. But you are ignoring the lesson because you have a hot tip: Buy Monday's opening. But if the crowd is buying on Monday's open, what will I be doing? Selling. And great will be the downdraft when the crowd (you and your reading friends following my hot tip) tries to get out of this trade. If you would be a trader, you must gain an appreciation for this point.

We are a little bit ahead of ourselves, so let me back up and give some clarification. It is common knowledge that everyone pays far too much attention to "hot tips" from the floor. You must know by now the conventional wisdom that those tips are worse than worthless; they are dangerous. Of course, these days, trading from the computer, you get the "advantage" of cable news. How's that working for you? This is why many a trader does not want to be confused by the news.

This one is a quaint saying, not a hot tip. And for many a beginner, this could be the most important lesson to come from the floor. Thus we have devoted an entire chapter to this sage line. If the concept is new, or you have even a slight discomfort with it, you are a novice; stay with us.

The crowd once believed that the world was flat. Great progress was made when a few took the opposing view. Now that the crowd believes that the world is round, we do not

---

[28] For the beginner—a stop is an order to buy *above* the market or sell *below* the market, but the order will not be filled, executed, until the market reaches your designated stopping price. Often called a stop-loss order. This could be the most important order for your to understand and use.

propose that round is a mistake. We are not saying that any commonly held belief is wrong. Nor are we simply anti-social, as has been often claimed. Nor do we play devil's advocate for the pleasure of disrupting a discussion, although that's been done too.

This maxim does not apply to truth. The truth does not become false as soon as the crowd believes it. Although I strongly recommend questioning all ideas considered to be true by virtue of their general acceptance. But that is another book.[29]

Truth is *never* affected by the opinion of the crowd. Price is *always* affected by the opinion of the crowd, because price is nothing more than an indicator of the balance between supply and demand at any given moment. And the crowd's opinion has always, and will always, have a very deceptive effect on demand. That effect will always move the price away from where it belongs. When the crowd is buying condos they won't live in and can't rent, what do you think will happen to the price of condos? Of course you know the extremes; the crowd bid up the price of tulips higher than their own homes.

Let's try an example closer to home. You come out of your house on your tenth birthday. You expected a raise in your allowance which has not happened and you're crushed. You look left and right. Every kid on your block has a lemonade stand in their yard. You say to your buddy next door, "What's the best way to make a little extra spending money?"

He gives you the conventional wisdom, "Listen pal. Lemonade is working. Don't even think about mowing lawns."

If you follow this crowd, you will spend the rest of your business life adding to the oversupply. I don't care if lemonade

---

[29] Thomas Payne said, "A long habit of not thinking a thing wrong, gives it a superficial appearance of being right." If you never trade, but can learn this maxim, you will look back on this moment as a key pivot point. The questioning of long held opinions is at the heart of human progress. And my emphasis is on "opinions." I stress this point because you, reading as you are in this footnote, have the quintessential inquisitive mind that will take even a wrong idea and use it to make something of value. That is creativity and don't you ever give it up.

is profitable. If everyone is doing it, I advise you to work on a recipe for hot chocolate. If everyone is selling Cadillacs, you should sell Volkswagens. If everyone is selling cars, you should sell gasoline. If everyone is selling transportation, you should sell food. (Those car-salespeople gotta eat.) I already mentioned the classic for the ages, wisdom from my father: If everyone is stampeding after gold, the quickest route to a fortune is to sell pics and shovels. This is not anti-social behavior. It is sound business practice.

If you can focus on supply and demand, you will easily see the point. Anything that the crowd is selling is underpriced; buy it. Anything that the crowd is buying is overpriced; sell it. I used to say that the bulk of the money I've made in this business (say 80 percent) was made this way. Every time I reflect on this point, I raise that percentage. These days my estimate is closer to a hundred.

It may take you a little while to absorb this point, and a little longer to put it into practice. If you picked up this book and read this far, you are most likely inclined to resist the crowd in the first place. If you are so inclined, you surely know why I have not included any "secret" entry and exit points. Here's that topic again. You are not in this business to copy others. You are here to make your own contribution to our economy.

Allow a few more practical examples. National news media outlets recently reported a crisis in an African country. You don't need the details; our focus is elsewhere. Weeks before the report, a concerned citizen had created a website to let people know about the situation. The website went viral and one of America's world-renowned leaders got behind the effort. Neither this leader nor the news media needed a website to inform them of the situation. They had known about it before. But because they are classic followers, they had done nothing until the website went viral and the crowd demanded action. Like most of us, they monitor the crowd and follow. I am a strong advocate of that old maxim—you get three options: 1) Lead, 2) Follow, or

3) Get out of the way.[30] In our country some people get more education than they need, become pundits, follow the crowd, and make a good living criticizing every leader who tries to make a difference. What a country! But for the rest of us, we have only these three options. I will not criticize those of you who freely chose to follow the crowd. But crowd-following and trading have a similar safety rating as vodka and driving. They will work well enough for a while. Then one day they won't.

Let's consider a common issue and see how it may apply. Currently we have a move to raise the minimum wage. How can any compassionate person argue against that? Some are even appealing to Jesus for support. We all desire for every worker to make as much as humanly possible. Why not? Naturally, the problem is far more complex than that, and not the purview of this book. But it is the generally accepted assumption that we should consider for a moment. We all assume that the closing of the gap between rich and poor is a good thing. Surely raising the minimum wage will do that. It has to. Even if there is a little inflation as a result, at least those on the minimum wage will gain. If the wealthy are hurt, we may take some small comfort in the closing of that gap. Surely the wealthy can afford it, and those who are generous will applaud it. After all, if America is famous for anything, we are famous for the emergence of a broad middle class that has done very well.

Do you have this picture? Now remember, as traders, our job is to question whatever the crowd accepts. And in this illustration the generally accepted truth, almost universally agreed upon, is that the gap between rich and poor should be reduced. Common knowledge, you say. So does everyone. Fine. To repeat,

---

[30] The line has been attributed to the great General George Patton. Thus one could easily imagine that he actually said, "Get the hell out of the way." He was so tough and so inspiring that his prayer life and wisdom have gone unnoticed. When referring to the scriptures he said that he read them "every god-damn day." He said a person need only concentrate on three things: Plan, work, and pray. When you feel yourself sliding into a follow-the-crowd rut, follow this man's example.

let us give at least a moment's consideration to the opposite of anything that the crowd accepts as a given. This could lead us to preposterous notions, but let's try it anyway and we'll keep quiet if we come up with lunacy. Here is the contrarian view: The gap between rich and poor is a good thing and should be expanded. I can almost see you cringing at the thought. But we won't die if we merely contemplate it for a moment. And don't tell anyone.

Let us suppose for example, that Bill Gates invented a piece of software that could make any of us a million dollars. It will cost each of us $50,000 to buy it, but the payoff will be a million. Anyone who can afford this software will rush out and buy it. Borrow the money if you have to, but get it. Indeed, most of us are using daily (me right now) some piece of software that is making us money by virtue of making us more efficient. And remember that Bill Gates has plenty of money, more than any of us. After we buy his software and make a million with it, what do you guess will happen to the income gap between us and Bill? I promise you that Bill will make more than a million with this software. He will make at least another billion, maybe ten.

If our commonly held maxim is accurate, we should stop Gates from developing that software or at the very least, boycott it when it comes out. If we don't, we will all participate in widening the gap between the rich and the poor. The gap between us and Bill will widen. And the gap between us and everyone who could not afford the software will also widen.

So let's reconsider: Maybe we should not close the gap between the rich and the poor. Maybe we should widen it. Naturally, you are welcome to disagree with anything in this book. But for now, please give serious consideration to my premise: Questioning the generally accepted assumptions of the crowd is not antisocial behavior. It is creative thinking. The fact that the crowd tells you it is antisocial behavior serves to illustrate, if not prove, my point.

Here's how to tell you are on the right track. Sooner or later you will hear someone ask about your idea, "If your idea is so great, why isn't everyone doing it?" Then you will know you are thinking like a trader. This is the classic put-down of any creative idea. It's the battle cry of mediocrity.

We have been taught that the great minds of the inventors are anomalies, the Edisons and the Fords of the world, that diligent, hard-working people do not think like them. Such critics are setting up to inform you that you are no Edison; you are no Henry Ford. You may even notice, if you watch very closely, that they are overcome with a tinge of satisfaction by so informing you. And what do *I* say? Please do not listen to these people. And when many of your attempts fail, which they will, these people will be there to gently observe with a reminding attitude. So let me remind you of something they will never notice. If Edison had listened to them, you would be reaching right now to adjust the wick on your whale-oil lamp. If they had been around to give Ford their sophomoric wisdom, you would have stopped reading a chapter back in order to go out and feed the horses. The sad fact is that unless you were lucky enough to have been born into wealth, you would feed someone else's horses. Some of you suppose that these past three sentences are exaggerations by an imaginative writer; you are thinking like the crowd. Please reconsider.

You have been given many invitations to leave this industry. And there will be more. But do not give up your creative, imaginative mind. Do not. Do not listen to those imparting their wisdom that it can't be done. They will never accomplish anything and get depressed if you prove them wrong. So go after it. Git 'r done. Make 'em depressed.

Even if you take one of my many invitations to find another profession, you still ought not be a crowd-follower. If you are, stop it. Do you need a history lesson? The success of the West in general and America in particular is due to the freedom everyone has had to take a road less traveled. Decide now to keep that tradition going.[31] Your willingness to go against the crowd will serve you well.

COROLLARY

For many of you, this analysis of the crowd is a review. Fine. But now an important corollary. You must be able to disagree with, and trade against, people who are smarter than you. I'm shaking my head as I write at the austere significance of the thought; it comes from me and I know that I don't have the IQ to give it any gravitas. So you are left to judge its importance on your own.

When I started out in the business, I had the premonition that this might be true. After a decade of trading, I began to have more confidence in it. After two decades, I was totally

---

[31] Americans are so complacent on this topic that they never notice the value of freedom, a fundamentally Judeo-Christian concept. Some of you will think that this book is little more than a Christian apology, an evangelistic attempt to convert people. There may be a tinge of truth in that. It is true that if you are a Christian, you will be much better prepared for the reality of chapter four and the trauma of chapter five. In fact this is not an apology; it is an attempt to get you prepared for the world of trading, and that means the world of drawdowns. Most of my readers will not have spent enough time in other parts of the world to notice that in America you can be whatever you want to be. You can be whatever faith you like, whatever denomination you like, an atheist if you like. All of this is meaningless academic theory to most Americans. Many are now embarrassed to admit that we started a revolution by asserting that these freedoms were a gift from God himself. The thought back then was that it was God who had given us the freedom to be an atheist, to curse him when we hit our thumbs with a hammer, and break most of the other commandments too. America has become great by protecting these God-ordained freedoms. You and I benefit from this freedom by being able to trade without the oppression that would be commonly experienced by the plebeians in most of the rest of the world. If you cannot agree with this point, you have had the extreme disadvantage of having had no experience in the third world. Put simply, you don't know how the other half lives. That saying alone demonstrates the naiveté about which I write. Half? Are you kidding? Half of the world is not in your class. Not close to half. That constitutes a wild assumption on my part about your class. Is it close? This is what we do when we trade—we make assumptions, calculate the odds, and invest when they favor us.

convinced. After three decades, I fell in love with the idea. And by now, I feel like it is indispensable to your success.

It is fair to assume that those who have extremely high IQs (let us suppose much higher than yours or mine) are right far more often than those with an average IQ. But they are not always right. The inclination to place confidence in these superior thinkers is pernicious in the extreme. It has led many a long way down a dangerous path. (That was a horrendous understatement.)

We simple folk talk about not being able to see the forest for the trees. Geniuses have a similar but greater problem; they miss the real problem because they focus cogently on matters that are off-topic or beside the point. And this often requires wisdom which they sometimes lack.

While doing a book tour with a Yanomami Indian, we had the privilege of visiting Reed College, a prestigious institution in Oregon. During the Q & A, I made an off-handed remark about teaching the Indians the concept of creating wealth. It appeared that the majority of the audience was shocked at my unabashed goal to pervert a utopian culture into a capitalistic, greedy, self-absorbed people. One questioner was so distraught that his facial features caused my Indian friend to give him a special nickname.[32] There was little I could do to recover from the open admission that I held productivity in high regard.

Seeing that I was getting nowhere, and my audience growing agitated, my Yanomami friend said, "I know you foreigners like to go fishing. And if you catch nothing, you stop at MacDonald's on the way home." That was a surprise; he had been quite observant on his short visit to the U.S. He continued, "When we Yanomami go fishing and catch nothing, on the way home we think about how we will not sleep all night because our children will cry from hunger."

A crowd of geniuses is not easy to read, so I don't know if he changed any minds. One thing is fairly certain, if we had all

---

[32] You do anything out of the ordinary and an Indian will give you a nickname. It will stick on you until you top it with another extraordinary move.

been given an IQ test, my Indian friend and I would not have ranked very high. This crowd was well convinced that capitalism breeds greed and is bad, and hunter-gatherers are simple forest dwellers and are good. Geniuses follow crowds too.

And while we may not have changed their minds, I promise you that they did not change ours. I still believe that children crawling on dirt floors while playing with their own mucus and bugs is not a hunter-gatherer's utopia.[33]

The horrendous difference of opinion I have just described is an example of a life-long conundrum. It is the tension, if we may call it that, existing between IQ and wisdom. Allow me one more story before considering this problem in more detail.

Please don't ask me how this one happened, but quite by accident I overheard a group of highly successful traders discussing the promotion of an employee to a coveted position that he sought. It may have been head trader or partner, something quite significant. One of the most respected of these traders made the argument that because this person was African-American, he was likely to be right-brained, and right-brained people do not tend to make good traders. Why would anyone commit a lot of capital in a high-risk situation after that analysis? None of the brilliant traders in the room, multimillionaires all, raised an objection.

Do you need more or can I rest my case now? For brevity sake, let's reduce the argument to its premises.

Right-brained[34] people do not make good traders.

African-American people tend to be right-brained.

This person is African-American.

---

[33] The world-renowned anthropologist, Napoleon Chagnon's popularized version of his bestseller is titled, *The Last Days of Eden*. Shoefoot, great leader of his village, has referred to that title as a mockery of his people. Check it out. Chagnon trashes the title (which he blamed on an ignorant publisher) in his introduction to the book.

[34] If you are like me, you don't care about half-brained analysis. I admit I had to look it up. Right-brained people cry, comfort the family, and write a poem to honor the memory of a friend when they are killed in an accident. Left-brained people try to figure out how it happened, who's to blame, and how it can be prevented in the future.

Q.E.D., he is probably not right for the job.

In the event that you, or any left-brained analyst, is interested in a reaction, allow me a short response to this argument that went unchallenged in that group of brainiac traders:

Right-brained people don't make good traders:

Every experienced trader knows that no one knows what makes a good trader. The left brain may dominate when it comes to trading, if you buy that whole left-right analysis. But I would not recommend trading with half a brain.

African-Americans tend to be right-brained:

Sweeping generalizations about a race are doubtful at best and seldom apply to a single individual; some white guys *can* jump. Have you ever been lumped into a category and had judgments made as a result? Welcome to the human race.

He's African-American:

No one knows the precise genetic linage of most dark people in America, especially those descended from slaves. He might be loaded with left-brained, European DNA for all we know.

Q.E.D.? Are you kidding? Three laughable premises leading to a Q.E.D.? The only thing proven by this argument is that I have been right all along: Geniuses can make mistakes too. Get used to this and do not hesitate to take market positions opposite them.

There is a side issue in this story that applies to trading. Most of you who are members of any minority race may be offended that I've told this story without using the words *racist* or *racism*. If this offends you or makes you angry, I need to pose you a question: Did you set aside your emotional reaction and focus on the individual premises? If you had a problem there, you must review this situation. Because when you trade, you must develop tunnel vision on the numbers, the facts, and the probabilities. You cannot allow yourself the luxury of distraction either with anger (in the case of a loss) or euphoria (when riding a winner). The geniuses will argue that the foregoing is left-brained analysis. So what? It's true.

It is not my intention to trash those of you with high IQs. If you have one, God bless you. Some of you have already decided that I'm an anti-intellectual with an ax to grind against the brainiacs. I'll let that go for now in the interest of focusing on the next problem we need to consider.

The problem is the relationship between IQ and wisdom. I hope to have proven that you do not need a high IQ to trade and you must be able to trade against those who are better traders than you. And now I complicate the issue by claiming that you cannot trade without wisdom.

All my life I've been pondering the mysterious relationship between wisdom and IQ. Back in high school we had a classmate who possessed an indisputable IQ of which all of us were jealous. On one outing of the Boy Scouts he took his bugle and blew it into a mud puddle. IQ he had. Wisdom? My classmates and I are still debating the point, while mostly we prefer to take joy at the memories he provided.[35] You will be interested to note that he went to the exclusive Reed College mentioned in the story a few pages back. (Next time I see him at our class reunion, I will ask if he took his bugle.)

In the history of thought, IQ is a relatively recent concept. And in my opinion the whole process is suspect. Certain minorities finally figured this out a few years ago when they noticed that the questions were set in subcultures with which their children were unfamiliar.[36] Thus the test favored those who had been raised in the subculture of the test designer.

---

[35] Senior Modern Issues class and the teacher mentioned a trite saying that was still appropriate in the 60s—that the Chinese were reproducing so fast that they could march four-abreast over a cliff and never reduce their population. Our classmate muttered, "How could they reproduce while marching four-abreast?" Mr. Wilson turned red and made little attempt to recover control of the class.

[36] Try this IQ test question: A guy has a girlfriend in the city and another girlfriend in the suburbs. The bus to the city goes by his house every ten minutes. And the bus going the other way to the 'burbs also goes by his house and also is on a ten minute schedule. So this guy figures he will walk out of his house, take the first bus to come along and thus let fate decide which girlfriend to visit, thinking to himself that over time he'll visit them both about equally. (Remember now, it is *your* IQ being tested, not his). But after a few months he finds himself growing much closer

But for our purposes, I've made the point that IQ is not the most critical aspect to trading anyway, and wisdom is indispensable. While openly admitting my own struggle with this topic, allow me to introduce you to the book of Proverbs. In fact, read it in the Complete Jewish Bible; it's closer to the original. Try to remember that this scripture is borrowed by us Christians from the original Jewish holy writ, word for word.

Naturally, some readers are thinking that this belongs in the FYX section. Not so. The book of Proverbs applies to everyone, no matter what your spiritual orientation. It's a little like the golden rule; we like people to live by it whether atheist or Hindu. The lessons of Proverbs have the same universal appeal. The importance of this book for the trader is that it will elevate wisdom. And it does so while almost overlooking the matter of IQ. Indeed, it introduces a critical third element, that of discipline.

Consider for a moment these lines from the opening chapter of Proverbs. See if you can identify how they apply to trading. We have not yet arrived at the holy grail coming up in the next chapter. But we are very close to it. It is common to see geniuses go belly up in the market. They do this by ignoring a very simple principle introduced in this opening chapter of Proverbs.

1. The proverbs of Shlomo the son of David, king of Isra'el,
2. are for learning about wisdom and discipline; for understanding words expressing deep insight;
3. for gaining an intelligently disciplined life, doing what is right, just and fair;
4. for endowing with caution those who don't think and the young person with knowledge and discretion.

---

to his city girlfriend and his 'burbs girlfriend is hot (not the good kind of hot—she's steamed). In fact, she discovers that he has visited his city woman nine times out of ten. She's ready to do the dumping. How did this happen? If you haven't figured this one out by now, it is only because you have little experience with buses and schedules. The test question is unfairly slanted in favor of those who have such experience. The point: Let the IQ test creators administer their tests to each other. This will give you and me more time to use our brains in more productive ways.

[5.] Someone who is already wise will hear and learn still more; someone who already understands will gain the ability to counsel well;

[6.] he will understand proverbs, obscure expressions, the sayings and riddles of the wise.

[7.] The fear of Adonai is the beginning of knowledge, but fools despise wisdom and discipline.

No doubt you've heard by now about the big three, the three traits you must have to trade: Discipline, discipline, and—what else? It's another one of those hot tips from the floor. But this time it is worth something.

The greatest system in the world (insert "wisest" or "smartest" or whatever word bolsters your confidence) will have times when it needs to be stopped out. Only a disciplined approach will get you out. Your high IQ might even battle against you with a variety of very intelligent reasons why you shouldn't take the loss.[37] Discipline will override any IQ and get you out of the market. That principle will cover the main body of this book; it is driving my editors mad with repetition, redundancy, déjà vu (all over again), and etcetera—in every chapter. It is at the core of all we do. It will surface again in the FYX section so you can see the spiritual foundation of the concept. Wisdom (or IQ, take your pick) has always and will always, get all the praise; but discipline gets the job done.

If you cannot get yourself married to this concept, namely, discipline trumps brain power, stop reading now and get yourself another line of work. You'll thank me later.

Having an ordinary intelligence quotient will not keep you from coming up with an extraordinary idea. You can take that to the bank. Intelligent people come up with great ideas because they know they can. And now you know you can too. Ordinary people like you and me (okay, let's not insult ourselves unnecessarily—let's say "slightly less than genius people like us") have grown to accept the following assumption: If there were a better

---

[37] Proverbs 26:12

way of doing this work, someone smarter than us would have thought of it long ago. On the basis of that assumption, we conclude that it is a "waste" of our brain to think of a better way to do it. Thus our brain becomes lazy, comfortable with the status quo, and follows the crowd into a rut. If we do have a creative thought once in a while, someone asks us who we think we are. And if we dare to give any sort of an answer, they remind us that we are not Thomas Edison, and we consume the humble pie and get back in the rut with the rest of the crowd.

The aforementioned mentality may have its place in the military, some assembly line procedures, and who knows where else. All one needs in a team effort is a creative non-conformist to muck up the best-laid plan. But when it comes to trading, the strategy of conformity to the status quo and following the crowd? Fu'get about it. (Chicagoese)

Surely you have heard this one; it's become a virtual cliché by now: Einstein defined insanity as doing the same thing over and over and expecting a different result. According to our crowd-is-always-wrong rule, you must never hold back on your suspicion of anything that becomes a cliché. Nothing turns wisdom into a cliché faster than a crowd. Please do me the honor of avoiding the repetition of these clichés. In our business, you will find yourself doing exactly what Einstein defined as insanity—you will do the same thing over and over.[38] And not only will you *expect* a different result, you will *get* a different result. Suppose you buy a breakout three times in a row and get stopped out for a small loss each time. What do you guess will happen if you "get smart," while quoting Einstein to yourself,

---

[38] I've never met anyone in our business who would take offense at this insanity insult. Everyone knows that the line between brilliance and lunacy is a poorly defined no-man's land. We walk it for the sheer joy of crossing over on rare occasions. I once heard a Jewish scholar claim that if the starlight had not bent around the sun during that solar eclipse, Einstein would have gone down in history as, "another dumb Jew." If you are not willing to run that risk, get out of this business.

and take a pass on the next breakout? Alright then—you're getting this business figured out.[39]

Most people who quote Einstein have no idea what he was talking about. The words of the wise in the mouth of a jester make for comedy, not wisdom.[40] Quote as many geniuses as required to bolster your confidence; but when you're finished, do your own thinking.

---

[39] If you didn't "guess what will happen," you are certainly a beginner. No shame in that; we'll summarize it for you. Buying a breakout is the purchase of anything when it breaks through some recent (usually arbitrarily defined) high (or low, in that case, selling). And the reason it breaks out and never looks back on the time you didn't buy it is because all the weak hands (you, and others who don't really want it), have gotten "smart," and refused to buy it on the fourth try. Thus it takes off and doesn't retrace because there are no close sell stops (placed there by you and the other weak hands) in the market to cause it to sputter.

[40] Proverbs abound on this point, Prov. 1:24-26; 26:7.

FYX

Good grief! How elementary. Who of you need me to clarify this? Could scripture make it any more obvious, squarely in my corner? "The gate that leads to destruction is wide and the road broad, and the crowd is on it."[41] Any questions?

This quote, reported by Matthew, should qualify as one of the most horrible lines of all antiquity. But there's more—a lot more: "Don't let the world around you squeeze you into its own mold, but let God re-mold your minds..."[42] Give your pastor this chapter and ask him to preach on this verse again. If you want to be a trader, don't hesitate for a minute to do a little mental remolding. And if you can get God to do it for you, all the better.

This is one of those advantages referred to earlier that Christians have; we are accustomed to going against the crowd. If you are not so accustomed, you may want to review your relationship with God. This trait ought to be a habit. You must have noticed that contemporary Christians have begun to lose this art. That is sad for reasons that have nothing to do with trading.

Neither did you need me to tell you that the path of the righteous is lonely. So what? We Christians are still going to face the problem that we do not have the luxury of running a Ponzi scheme, leaning on orders, front running, or other unscrupulous activities.[43]

However, this chapter is not about the lonely road of righteousness. We are speaking of the lonely road of creative

---

[41] Mt 7:13. It is CJB, however, I admit adding "the crowd," when CJB and most other translations render, "many." But I feel we can agree that Jesus' use of "many" surely implies a crowd.

[42] Romans 12:2. This rendering by J.B. Phillips has not been disputed by any scholar to my knowledge and it surely captures the emotional angst produced by a commercially manipulated culture.

[43] Don't anyone suppose that Christians have not done all these things. Our track record here is disgusting. Jesus must be so ashamed, and busy on judgment day.

thought. Yet even on this topic holy writ still overflows with illustrative material.

Mrs. Noah was overheard, "For just once could you try to be like everyone else?"

Moses to his tyrant, "How about giving your slaves a few days vacation?"

Samson to his guard, "I could sure use a bigger column to lean against."

Sarah to Abraham, "I laughed because those guys are naive and ignorant; my headache never goes away."

Joshua to everyone, "Let's get some exercise and hike around Jericho."

John to Herod, "How do you think your brother likes you messing with his woman?"

The mysterious thing about the scripture is not the stories that stagger credulity, Jonah's fishy tale, etc. The magic of scripture is the stories of ordinary people who were so focused on God that they forgot about their comfort zone. I've given you the short list. You can find the rest. But let me conclude the point with the mother of all nonconformist lines—the Apostle Paul overheard asking, "Why don't we try this Jewish atonement idea on the Goyim?"[44]

Now the bad news for the believer: We have a built-in respect for those in spiritual authority over us. People in spiritual authority have called me greedy, scrooge, loose cannon, traitor, worshiping at the altar of the dollar, and more—some of it

---

[44] I'll never forget my surprise when hearing my history prof at Portland State University say that no single person had altered the course of human history more than the Apostle Paul. A few scholars have gone so far as to call Christianity, Paulinism. These scholars get approximately the quantity of respect that their view deserves, about an ounce, which explains why you have never heard of it. I mention it merely to speculate whether it is possible for an Apostle to turn over in his grave. Cf, Acts 22:21. "But he said, 'Get going! For I am going to send you far away — to the Goyim!'" (That is an unaltered quote from holy writ, *Complete Jewish Bible*.) But the important point you must not miss is the crowd's reaction. "They shouted at the top of their lungs, 'Rid the earth of such a man! He's not fit to live!'" (v.22) If going against the crowd were easy, everyone would be a trader.

publicly. And the Catholics have it far worse than we Protestants. Some Catholics believe that their church has the power to decide their eternal destiny. Protestants never had it so good. Thus, we have no excuse for allowing ourselves to be manipulated by those in spiritual authority. But alas, alack, we fail anyway.

Obviously the easy example for this is Jim Jones and his deceived followers. One can hear on the tape a few lone voices trying to offer Jones an alternative. When you've followed the guru that far in search of spiritual bliss, you are in deep trouble. But the Jones mass suicide, and murder, is far too simple and extreme an example. And what is worse, it represents what we all know as 20-20 hindsight. In the trading business, everybody can see those "obvious" trades when looking backward.

So let me give you an example more like what an ordinary Christian will surely face. (And for you non-believers who keep sneaking in here without permission, take a hike now—this is *so* embarrassing. You'll never hear a Christian brag on this stuff.[45])

A leading elder of my church once pointed his finger at me and said, "If you leave this church, God's hand of protection will be lifted off of you." For those of you who think I've wandered far from trading, think again. When you walk into the pit every morning, hear the bell ring, and know that one courageous trade that is too large could take you down, you take "the hand of God's protection," pretty seriously. (BTW, you need not be in our business to have the same fear. How many of you text while driving?)

So there it is, a theological pronouncement, God's hand of protection coming off of Mark Ritchie. And he accompanied

---

[45] This is an incredibly important point for you non-believers who insist on getting this horrible inside info. You think that these Christian-hypocrisy stories disprove our faith. If they did, Christianity would have been eradicated when they dug up Wycliffe in order to do the "righteous" thing; they burned his corpse at the stake. I remind you that the Jewish carpenter taught that these "Christian" preachers are going to hell. It was no parable about what might happen. I will die a happy man if you non-believers can find a way to avoid meeting them there. (cf. Matthew 25:31ff. You'll know you're suckin' air when you hear some guy say, "Line up with those goats on the left.")

the "statement"[46] with a popular theological diagram quickly drawn up on the whiteboard. The diagram showed an umbrella (representing the church, God's instrument of protection), the rain coming down (representing the trials of life, e.g., market locked limit down against my position—for days), and stick-people safely under the umbrella (representing those who stay in his church). Then of course he adds another stick-man, Mark Ritchie, out in the rain getting soaked; that would be me leaving his church.

Because you haven't noticed the umbrella picture in holy writ, you may be curious to know its origin. In my first book I told the story of my romance and how I won my woman away from a "wonderful" Christian ministry and its leader. Everyone who knew the Christian community of that time recognized the organization and its seminar. Spiritual manipulation and control were a part of what was called God's "chain of command." The charismatic leader wanted Nancy to dump me and serve his ministry. Have you noticed that these spiritual leaders almost always come up with scenarios that are advantageous to them?

The story would be long past sour grapes and not worthy of mentioning were it not for the fact that I got a call from that very seminar teacher recently. He wanted to apologize about that ancient story, admit that it was his fault, and ask for forgiveness. I said, "Sir, we had this conversation forty years ago and there was not an ounce of humility in your tone, no apology on your lips, and a judgmental lecture for me."

He said, "God has taught me a lot over the past forty years and I'm sorry for my attitude back then." Now it is not my goal here to evaluate the sincerity of this well-known leader. Let's leave that to others, if not God. The truth is that all these leaders started out to serve the Lord; but they refuse to listen to anyone along the way. And why would any spiritual giant ever listen to a person like me, one who uses "unrighteous

---

[46] I have selected the most innocuous word I can think of, "statement." But pronouncement, threat, prophecy, edict, are also possible. Pick your own noun. There is a lot of latitude for interpretation.

mammon" (cash) as his raw material. That would require a level of humility with which they are not blessed. So they end up forty years down the road asking for forgiveness, which of course, no Christian is permitted to withhold.

To give an ounce of gravitas to this theme, in the unlikely event that there is a member of the clergy who has not yet tossed this book into his garbage, let me appeal to the great theologian, John H. Gerstner. He said that the more righteous a man is, the more pernicious his errors become, because his followers would never run the risk of rebelling against a righteous elder. These spiritual giants clothe themselves with pious mannerisms, often designated as "Christ-like." If they ever saw me trading in the pit, they would say, "That guy is the poster-boy for non-Christian demeanor." This is because they do not understand the story of the violent removal of the traders from the temple courtyard. Do they need me to remind them that the story was not a parable? It happened. If Jesus followed their mild-mannered example, he would have "ministered" to the poor, teaching them insights about freeing your inner spiritual person by forgiving those money-changing cheats.[47]

The parishioners at Westboro Baptist Church are able to walk around with signs reading, "God Hates Gays," because they have a God-fearing preacher who has misled them in that direction. We Christians are uniquely susceptible to being misled by these spiritual giants, if we want to call them that. Nevertheless, I maintain my thesis and request that you give it consideration: It is possible for those more spiritually mature than you to

---

[47] Scholars are still debating whether Jesus did this twice or whether John's account was a flash-forward. (John 2:13f; Matt 21:13f; Mk 11:15; Lk 19:45) I'm a trader with a highly negative attitude about unscrupulous markets. So I will admit to being strongly prejudiced in favor of the interpretation that has Jesus doing this twice. For all we know, he may have done it more often. In John's story he rebuked them for turning the father's house into a market, which one might guess implies, "Who's gonna clean up all this fecal matter?" And in the other stories he accuses them of being a den of thieves. I wonder how he might clean up some of our order-filling habits.

be wrong.[48] Just look at Galatians 2:11,12 where Paul opposed all the Christian leaders for their mistake of racial segregation. And while we are on that topic, let me suggest the greatest poster-person to illustrate the point, the great General Robert E. Lee. No one doubts that he was a spiritual giant. No one doubts that he was a brilliant general. We don't know his precise IQ, but the assumption that it was very high is safe. But he was mistaken. And his leadership was costly.

You may have already noted the shortage of Christian leaders who have endorsed this book. That is because although they may be more respected than us, more intelligent than us, more spiritually mature than us, they are still capable of making mistakes. Now why would they endorse a message like that?

This is enough dirty laundry. Let us return again to the point, and it is not theological. The theologians have merely provided the illustrative material. My point is that you must be able to trade on the opposite side of those who are smarter than you, disagree with those who are more spiritually mature than you, and refuse to allow the angst that they produce to distract you from your calling. I stood in the soybean meal pit at 9:29am getting my numbers ready for the opening bell; it was the morning following that elder's prophetic declaration. His umbrella picture and his pronouncement of God's judgment were not clouding my thinking. That elder went on to earn degrees in theology, write books, hold a professorship at a well-known seminary, and is today a significant spiritual leader. He merely made a mistake. That is all.

Just because you disagree with the crowd does not mean that you have to make your opinion known. You will surely tire of hearing that phrase, "loose cannon on deck." I will not tell you how often I've heard it. Trust me, it has never occurred to anyone who uses that "loose-cannon" line that their deck might have a few items God might want to clear off. If you are

---

[48] I am overloaded with illustrative material on this point and I refuse to bore you with it.

a cannon, do not bolt yourself down. (Anybody tired of this metaphor?)

But please weep not for me. Instead consider this: If the loose-cannon phrase has never been used on you, if you have a strong urge to go along with the crowd, if you cannot make waves, if you must fit in, if you resist embarrassment at any cost, if you must avoid every failing effort, it is likely that you are not ready for trading.

Please do not think that this business is all negative. We traders focus on our losers, that is true. But that is only because we will not enjoy the winners unless they considerably offset the losers. So let us close this chapter on a positive note, with a line from one of the greatest figures of antiquity, the Jewish psalm writer, David. He wrote, "I have more understanding than all my teachers, because I meditate on your instruction."[49]

If you are meditating on God's instructions, the golden rule for example, you will naturally avoid the mistake of following the crowd. I cannot explain how this will open your mind to new ideas. There is something novel about the approach. You will always be thinking along a different track. You will make a feeble attempt to think God's thoughts after him.[50] I admit that David's line about "knowing more than my teachers" elicits a smile from anyone who hears me quote it. But it's not a joke. Surely you've had teachers who weren't the sharpest tools in the woodshed; we all have. But we've had some great ones too. You can identify their greatness when you notice that their desire for you, their student, is that you exceed them in knowledge and achievement. I write this material so that you may far surpass me on your path to understanding trading and more.

So if you need to put your tongue in your cheek when you quote David's sage line, get it quoted. Then pray that God will write it on your life; he must answer that prayer if you are to become a successful trader.

---

[49] Ps 119:99 CJB

[50] Johannes Kepler gets the credit for this unusually artistic expression. But many scientists, Einstein among them, have made similar comments.

CHAPTER FOUR

THE HOLY GRAIL

I will often begin a lecture with the following game–or we'll call it what it is—a wager: I pop out half a dozen $100 bills and offer to lend them to anyone willing to play. Then here's the deal: I lend you this $100 bill. You will wager it, or any portion of it, on this quarter I am about to flip. You have a 50 percent chance of winning, obviously, a 50 percent chance of losing. Now, to make this a winning opportunity for you, the house, that's me, will reward you 120 percent of what you risk on your wager. And when you lose, naturally you lose 100 percent of what you risked. Got the picture? This is quite straightforward.[51]

If you have trouble identifying this as a winning proposition, please do your heirs a favor and look for another line of work. If you think this whole setup is a trick situation, back up one sentence and take me seriously. It is a substantial effort, not a joke. The same applies to an audience to which I speak. This is written to help the serious trader and save the 401k of

---

[51] It has been mentioned earlier that we will get more technical in this chapter. And while I have minimized the importance of IQ, let me assure you that if you have any difficulty following the principles of this chapter, it is not for lack of IQ. It is because your gifts lie outside the field of math. This is basic high school level arithmetic. If you got through algebra, you can get through this.

the wannabe who should be doing something more productive than trading.

Now don't be shy; step up and take the risk. Put your money where your mouth is—you can think up your own cliché to apply, thus saving me a little work.

We will grant that it does not duplicate the real world, but for our purposes at this point, it does. (More on this later) Right now I need you, my audience, to make your first investment. I've offered this identical investing opportunity to a wide variety of audiences and received a wide variety of responses. By *wide* I mean some have invested one dollar while others have shot the whole hundred. No doubt you'll agree; that is a wide variety. If we dispense with these outliers (one and a hundred), we still have a variety of opinions with which to experiment. In an audience situation, I tell them that whoever takes my $100 bill and makes the most money on this little investment strategy, gets to keep the money. Your speaker acts as the house and pays off any winnings. This is my way of making it more than a game. They stand to profit. So they take it seriously. It is no game.

Now you, the reader, are a member of my hypothetical audience. And I need you to get a real number in your head. We are simulating the real world as best we can on paper. (We'll discuss paper trading later.) So write the number down and let us begin. Manifestly, the most significant influence on your number is the amount of capital you have at your disposal. In my audience I lend them all $100 of my own money to invest. They will owe me the $100 back. But I will pay all winnings to the one who makes the most.

"Okay," I say, "you all have your number written down." And I flip the coin and catch it. But before I turn it over to reveal who won, I say, "Wait. Let us suppose that we remove the element of luck from this game." We know that the law of averages will neutralize luck over time. So let us suppose that I flip this coin about ten times and I assure you that you will win and lose an equal amount. Then I'll ask, "Does anyone wish to change the amount they invest on our first flip?"

Now I will ask you, the reader, to think that over a moment. Will you change your investment number now that you know that the law of averages is going to treat you as it should? In the game I described, there will always be someone who will invest $100 on the first flip to get a head start on the competition. "In fact," I say to my audience, "let's make this as real as possible. I will require you to increase your size after you win and decrease it after you lose, just like you would in real life." Thus your number becomes a percentage of the $100 bill you are using for your capital.

"Now," I say, "change your number if you wish, and stick with that as your percentage for every flip of the coin." So you, the reader, may wish to change your number. (I have not yet welcomed back to our reading group the pro traders who took my advice and skipped those first three chapters. But now we welcome them back. I mention these pro traders here because I doubt that a pro will change the amount to invest after hearing that the law of averages is going to be average. Why would they? We pro traders *always* expect the law of averages to be average. That's how it got its name.)

But you have your chance now, before the first flip, to change your number. You know how this is going to work. All you have to do is come up with some number that you will invest on this sure-fire winning system.

While you are thinking, I'll mention, as I always do, that this is no trick question. There is no intention on my part to pull a fast one. We traders make trades all day long, every day. If one could make a trade with these parameters each minute and could start with $100, one could make a million dollars by the end of the first week of trading. By the end of the second week, the trader will be able to pay off the national debt.[52] At the end of the third week, this trader could own everything in the world. I have not run these numbers in a while, so it is possible that a

---

[52] Well, actually, this is what I used to say. And it was true when I first began presenting the challenge. But in the years that have followed, the debt has risen to the point that one could not pay it off until Monday of the following week.

little inflation could require our fictional trader to work a few more days in order to purchase the rest of Russia. The point is that this is a very real and legitimate investing opportunity—not a mathematical trick.

Okay, I stand here ready to flip my fictional coin. How much of that $100 that I loaned you is on this opening flip? If you are serious about trading, you *must* answer this question before you move on. This is quite important. I'll admit to stalling for time here to force you to answer the question before you proceed. One questions I often get is, "How do you overcome the reluctance to pull the trigger on a trade?" It's a good question. One thing is sure, if you can't pull the trigger now, you never will. In the last seminar I did, the investments ranged from 5 to 75 percent.

Okay? I've stalled long enough. If you don't have a number by now, you've got other issues. Write it down here on the page so you can't change it later. You are working with a disadvantage. You see, my audience has a strong competitive incentive to maximize their return for the purpose of winning the cash I always offer to the winner. You, being a reader, will get nothing, save maybe the bragging rights of what you would have won. But the point is that there is no reward for being overly conservative. Everyone, game-player or trader, has the same goal—maximize profits.

If your number is on the page, let's see what would happen if you chose a relatively harmless 20 percent. I start there because this is a common choice, probably the most popular of all the audiences, and what I might have used at the black-jack table when I saw the cards tipping slightly in my favor.[53]

You must follow this; we are fast approaching the heart of the matter. Let us assume that you are successful on your first investment, i.e., you make $24. (A $20 investment returns 120 percent which equals $24.) Now you have $124 and you are

---

[53] It should be obvious that 20 percent comes out the same no matter what our original capital is–$20 on $100, or $20,000 on $100,000. Granted, everyone becomes more conservative as their capital grows; but let's set that principal aside for the present discussion.

ready to make more. You invest 20 percent on the next trade, which is $24.80. Now we will assume that you lose on this one, which leaves you with $99.20. If you have any natural gift for this business, you noticed in the middle of the sentence, two sentences back, that you were in trouble while traveling down this scenario. Because you know that one win and one loss is the proper amount of wins, just what you expect to achieve over time. And you are now behind where you started. You may assume that the outcome would vary were lady luck to treat you differently, say you lost on your first investment and then won the second. If that happened, you will have $80 left after the loss. Then you invest 20 percent of that $80 ($16) and you win. You gain 120 percent of $16 which equals $19.20. Now you have $99.20 left. This might be a good time to stop and feel the blood draining from you head.

Would you like to see this on a graph?

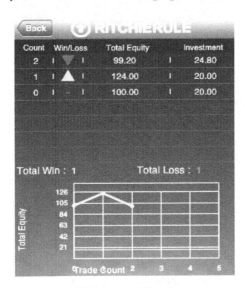

20 Percent Graph

You have now made two investments in this winning system. We didn't like the outcome when we won on the first one. So we asked lady luck to cut us some slack, let us lose on the first one, then win the second. But we came out *exactly* the same using that second scenario. Can anyone imagine a way to stop this sick trend?

Well, we've come this far, let's get crazy and try 50 percent. That'll show 'em what we're made of. We're the cowboys of the finance world. We know how to roll the dice with the big boys. (These metaphors proceed downhill. Insert your own.) If we invest $50 and win, we make $60 and have $160. Great. Now we invest 50 percent of 160, i.e., $80, and when we lose we have $80 remaining. We already know that changing the order will not affect the outcome. But you can run that on your own and you'll see; you'll still come out with $80. Have a look:

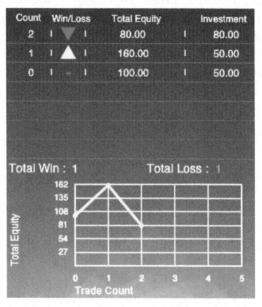

50 Percent Graph

Investing larger is clearly going the wrong direction. But before we move in the other direction, i.e., lower the percent that we invest, let's do a quick review. We tried two scenarios. In the first, at 20 percent, you lost 80 cents after two trades. In the second, we lost $20 after two trades. Even a novice trader knows that controlling your losses is one of the most important factors in trading. But look at the difference in these two examples. In the second we lost 25 times as much as in the first.

You should see it now, if not anticipating it coming, that your profit margin is affected more by your money management technique than by anything else. If you haven't paused to absorb that last sentence, do so now. If that sentence did not hit you like a ton of bricks, you haven't traded. I will belabor this point without apology and defend it against every editorial objection:

Your profit margin is affected more by your money management than by anything else.

Please emphasize "anything else." Because "anything else" is the primary topic of almost every other trading book on the market—and almost every other trading seminar and trading guru. You (the novice reader and my editors at Macmillan) have been showing how important "anything else" is every time you complain about my lack of entry and exit points.

You have now arrived as close to the holy grail of investing as you will ever get. You know that "holy grail" is a tongue-in-cheek phrase. I use it because we all know that everyone is looking for it, and every sane trader knows there is no such thing. Nevertheless, if you fail to pay attention here, you can be guaranteed to become a losing trader.

To further illustrate, if not prove the point, let us move in the other direction. Let's try investing 15 percent of our hundred dollars. We'll lose first, have $85 remaining. Then we invest .15 X 85, or 12.75. When we win, we get 12.75 X 1.2, = 15.30. We now have $100.30. Shake hands with yourself. You just turned a winning situation into a winning situation. If that last sentence confused you, join the club in the massive crowd of losing traders. The reason this crowd is so large is because they do not realize how easy it is to turn a winning situation into a losing situation. Your job is to turn a winner into a winner.

While we are headed in the right direction, why would we stop? We try 10 percent next. After our loss, we have $90 left. We invest 10 percent of $90 ($9) and win. (1.2 X 9 = $10.80) Thus we have $100.80 after the two trades. We made more at 10 percent than we made at 15 percent.

We better try 5 percent. We have $95 after the loss. We invest $4.75 and make 1.2 X $4.75, which is $5.70, giving us a total of $100.70.

Let's do 2 percent. We get $100.35. Clearly, this trend demands that we try something between 5 and 10 percent. So let's try 8. My numbers give me $100.83.

If these numbers are a bit hazy to you now, just look at this hand-drawn graph and the light will dawn.[54]

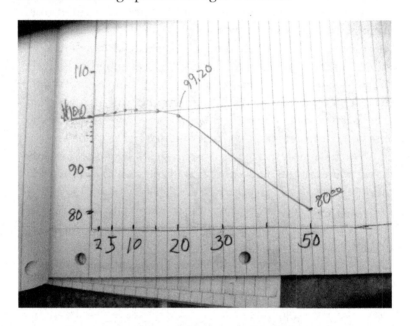

TOTAL EQUITY AFTER TWO TRADES
horizontal–percent to invest, vertical–total equity

This is it. You are witnessing the closest you will ever come to the holy grail of trading. There is no graph in our industry more important than this one. Please take as much time as you need

---

[54] I cannot pass this opportunity to stress the importance of thinking in pictures. I drew this chart yesterday, I knew what it would look like, and it still surprised me.

to understand this graph.[55] The horizontal axis is the percent you might decide to invest. The vertical represents your capital. We started with $100. So the graph represents our profit curve after two trades for each percent which we chose to invest. There is a huge quantity of space on the right side of this graph to accommodate the vast majority of traders. They all lose money. This is where the adrenaline flows, the big trading stories are made, and the smartest people in the room make fortunes when they are right. But eventually the law of averages catches up with them and they hit the skids. Then there is the left side of the graph, so minute as to look boring by comparison. (More to come on boredom.)

---

[55] First you should notice that the graph is nothing special. It is the result of a pencil, paper, and huge eraser. This is where most of the real work gets done. I could have done a fancy, computer-generated graph, but I want you to see that it's the thinking you do at the kitchen counter that makes the difference in your performance. I scribbled this chart out at the kitchen table, took a picture of it, and was again in awe when I saw the contrast between the two sides of the graph. I use a mechanical pencil with as much led as I can find. Hence the need for a big eraser. I use .7 mil led, have now found .9 mil led, and once found 2.1 mil led in Myanmar. The 2.1 mil pencil cost me $.30. I bought all they had.

First you need to have a look at the future of those who invested 50 percent and 20 percent.

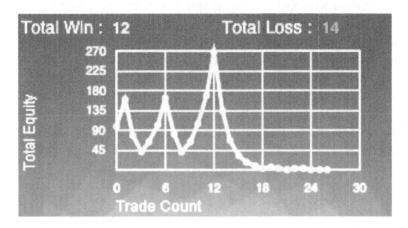

50 Percent Curve

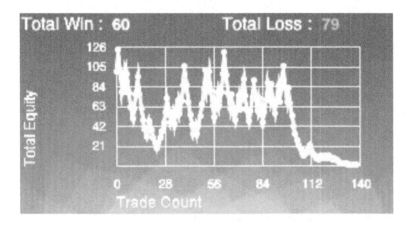

20 Percent Curve

You can see that neither of these traders goes broke right away. Nevertheless, the end is inevitable. And it will not matter how many times I try this scenario. Each one will be different. Each will deliver a payload of adrenaline along the way, because each will have its moments when the law of averages will make your entry points look great. You must notice that in the weaker scenario, the fifty percent curve, there was a nice run up. You almost tripled your money at one point (up to $270). Nothing will give you the cocktail party stories like that. You came home high-fiving your spouse. At that point everyone knew you were a genius. Even you started to believe it. But every scenario will end the same. I call this the holy grail because there are certain guarantees built into the systems laid out in this chapter. Some of the systems guarantee failure—every time. And it's only a matter of time. Others guarantee success.

You may have heard on occasion an investment sales person use this stat: Eighty percent of the people who invest in the financial markets lose money. Then they add their punch line, "That means that the other twenty percent make a fortune."

Let me assure you that anyone making such an observation possesses two important features: First, ignorance. And second, total trading inexperience. That is a mathematical stunt resulting in deception. If you look at the 20 percent graph above, you will notice periods of profit. Those periods of profit represent the trades of this semi-fictitious twenty percent of traders who suppose they are profitable in any specific year. But in the next year, the 20 percent who were profitable the year before join all the rest of the newcomers to the trading enterprise. It is only reasonable to us assume that the 80 percent have wised up and left. And that year 80 percent of the 20 percent winners from the year before, i.e., 16 percent, become losers in the current year. Get it? Over time, they all lose.

None of these stats apply to pro traders who are profitable year in and year out. And these stats mislead amateurs, a high percentage of whom fail year in and year out until they are all gone. The rate at which these people fail is of no interest to you or me. It could be 80 percent, but who cares? Of course there is new blood coming into the market each year, thanks to the efforts of talented salespeople who use such statistics to convince their clients that they know how to trade. In actual fact, if they knew how to trade, they would not need clients. The momentum of salespeople bringing new investment money into the market generally keeps this merry-go-round up and running. These salespeople and their clients have never seen that disastrous hand-drawn graph, are totally unfamiliar with this concept, and have a strong tendency to migrate over to the right side of the page. All this material is just as new to them as it is to you.

Pro traders, stick around for one more item, the Ritchie Rule, and you will have all that this book has to offer you. If you go online you can purchase the Ritchie Rule app. The charts generated in this chapter, with the exception of the hand-drawn one, are taken from this app. It will cost you a whopping $.99, my attempt to demonstrate that old maxim, *the best things in life are almost free*. Google "Ritchie Rule" and go from there. Currently, it is only programmed to work on the I-Phone and I-Pad (Android coming soon).

The RR will demonstrate the so-called holy grail in a video game format. When the RR opens, you see the page shown at the right. You are prompted to answer four very simple questions.

First: Start Up Capital– trading lingo for, "How much money are you willing to lose?" You won't need to learn the trading lingo, but you must have a good understanding of this number.[56] You'll see

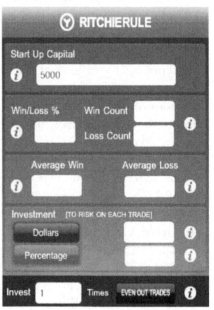

---

[56] No novice trader (nor many pros) has any understanding of this concept. None. They risk $10,000 and when they have lost $5,000, they quit, saying to themselves that discretion is the better part of valor, and equating the same with wisdom. Then it never occurs to them that they fooled themselves when they said they had risked $10,000. What they actually did was they flashed $10,000 as a display of gravitas to someone (almost always themselves), but they only risked $5,000. Yet they probably set their trading sizes as if they

that it is defaulted to $5,000. But you can click on it and adjust it to meet your requirements. (In our illustration, $100 goes here.)

Second: Win/Loss percentage. This is merely a statement of how often your investment is successful. If you win one time out of four, enter 25 percent in the first box, or one in the win count and 3 in the loss count. (In our illustration, 50 percent goes here.)

Third: Tell the Rule the size of your average win and your average loss. If you enter a size that can only win with luck, the RR will voice (print out) its disapproval of your system, but allow you to trade anyway (we call it gambling). (In our illustration, $12 for average win and $10 for average loss. This will simulate our situation.)

Fourth: Assuming you have a profitable system established, as our illustration is, now comes your last choice; how much will you invest (risk, that is) on each trade? Select either a dollar amount, and the RR will tell you the percent. Or select a percent, and RR will tell you the dollar amount.

There is one more box, the "invest" box at the bottom which will allow you to run more than one investment at a time. You should begin with one, which is the default. The option to "even out trades" will force the system to remove luck from the your venture, i.e., if you have a 25 percent win rate and ask for 10 trades, it will give you 12 trades with 3 wins and 9 losses. *However*, this option is *not yet functional*, so do not bother to try it.

Now that you pro traders have the RR, you are dismissed from class. You may want to visit the next chapter to get the formula behind the RR. You'll need that. The next chapter will

---

were risking $10,000. We are showing in this chapter that this mistake is fatal. And this mistake is made industry-wide. Account managers will even ask a client, "Would you like me to trade your $10,000 as if it were $20,000?" These people are account managers–not traders. A few will get lucky and do very well. But the clients who got caught in the downdraft of the right side of the graph will go away. And the account manager will have no trouble replacing them with new clients by showing any new client the track record of the few who made money. What a business!

also give you an appreciation for the severity of the downs we suffer, but you should need no reminder on that score.

For the rest of us, enjoy the game, apply it to any of your own trading numbers, and use it to learn what sort of profit curve your system may be likely to lead you down. Trading is no game, as you know, but sometimes it helps to treat it as a game; you don't want to focus on the actual number of dollars you are losing. That can be hopelessly distracting. The goal of RR is to give you an advance introduction to the ups and downs (mostly the downs) of trading a real market.[57] You will soon notice what has already been demonstrated—you can set up a winning system and still go broke, even without bad luck. Of course we are all geniuses when the law of averages swings our way.

If you know any pro traders, you may find some who will disagree with the entire premise of this chapter. If this chapter is wrong, the rest of this book is a house of cards. If they disagree, it is because they do not need the RR. Professional traders have the formula behind the RR built into their DNA. If they dispute me, I'll argue that a honeybee will claim to know nothing about a hexagon. That is not a writer's hyperbole; you can take it to the bank. If pro traders used percentages remotely similar to those of the novice, they would be going broke at about the same rate, which is preposterous. In my career I can only recall two pro traders who went broke.

We are now in the heart of the holy grail. Ask any failed trader[58] how his system has done after he stopped trading it. That's when you will hear the woulda-coulda-shoulda stories.

---

[57] You surely know by now that all we care about is the downs. Any fool can make money when the market cooperates; it takes talent to lose it. That might read like a quaint saying, but you better get married to it. We traders are not negative people. We just know that there is nothing to be positive about when you are broke. It should come as no surprise that what I have called the holy grail shows up where no one is looking; it comes on the negative side, i.e. it doesn't make money; it keeps you from going broke.

[58] Usually a good storyteller, in demand at cocktail parties for their abilities.

It is a rough estimate that 75 to 95 percent of all the woulda-coulda-shoulda stories in our business can be traced to a fundamental misunderstanding of this principle.

Just in case you need a review with simpler numbers. First you lose 50 percent. Then you make 75 percent. That feels like success. But when your accountant does the real numbers you end up a losing trader with 87.5 percent of what you started with.[59] You can, and you will, blame your entry and exit points. But the fact is that while you are doing all that work, tweaking your entry and exit points, talking about how much you would have made if you had continued, and on and on, you are overlooking this principle: You traded too large. And I do not mean that you were undercapitalized. There's another big mistake. It was not a lack of capital. If you had more capital, you would have traded larger. If you don't trade at the right size with little capital, you won't trade at the right size with more capital.[60]

The biggest disagreement that any trader will have with any of this material is the use of the phrase "holy grail." Pro traders will heap on the scorn. We all know that the search for the holy grail is the first sign of a novice, the beginner, the smartest-guy-in-the-room, the setup for failure. Nevertheless, I use the phrase because I know that without the concept you've encountered here, you cannot succeed in this business. Legendary system developer, Welles Wilder, found the holy grail a few decades back.[61] If there were a holy grail, it should be no

---

[59] If this is not quickly recognizable, you need to find a wing of this business that is not so numbers oriented. Then hire a numbers person to keep track of you.

[60] Does this remind you of your government? It should. They are the poster child for this problem. When their revenue (our taxes) goes up, confidence rises, spending rises, and our national debt also rises. I am not a gloom-and-doomer, but that will not keep the chickens from coming home to roost.

[61] For you younger guys, Welles Wilder is famous for the development of the Relative Strength Index, RSI. But then he got a little carried away. My friend, Austin Pryor, tells the story to top all stories about Wilder and the holy grail. Wilder came up with the ability to predict every turn in the market going out into forever. It was the most amazing discovery in the history of everything. I would never steal from Pryor the right to tell this story. And when you learn

surprise to find it hiding where no one is looking. This is where I found it.

Call it whatever you want—so long as you know that without a thorough understanding of this chapter and the next, you will fail in this business. You can take that to the bank too.

Surely this is all clear enough. There will be some of you who still suppose this is some sort of mathematical stunt. If you think that, back up and review. If, after that, you have not changed you mind, find another line of work.

For you who see the light, here's where the real problem comes—this conundrum is camouflaged by a market that never delivers our profits and losses in the neat package that we have seen with these numbers. Thus our focus remains on our entry and exit points. It keeps us analyzing the market, tweaking our thinking, maybe even analyzing ourselves, our inability to pull the trigger. We have so much opportunity for second-guessing with our "brilliant" hindsight that we can far overanalyze every turn in the market. "We didn't let that profit run long enough." "We needed a bigger stop." "We needed to cut that loss shorter." These speculations could fill another chapter. There is so much on which to focus that it never occurs to us to imagine that all our trading might be perfect; we just traded too large. That is all. Full stop. Finish. Save yourself all that analysis, not to mention grief and pain.

There will be some of you who will wonder why this author would give away the goose that is laying the golden egg. These may be the same people who complain that I never give away any entry points. Some pro traders may wonder the same. The answer: My profit (and that of any pro) is made from entry and exit points. YOU ARE NOT GETTING ANY OF THOSE AND YOU NEVER WILL. Your losses are made from your lack of understanding of the graphs presented in this chapter. If you adjust your trading to line up with these graphs, it will

---

what he paid for his grail, you'll know why Austin has exclusive rights to such story telling. Shocking, chilling, hilarious, and proof of what we all know: There is no holy grail. (Austin will tell you the story, if you can catch him in a mood to be laughed at. It is the ultimate, How-could-I-do-that, story.)

have no effect on my profitability, or on the profitability of any other pro trader.[62] It will only effect your profitability.

Now some of you will be asking what accounts for the profit—entries and exits, or money management? Or you will accuse me of withholding the real secrets—entries and exits.

Answer: Your entries and exits make you the money. You will discover these over time as you gain experience getting in and out of the market. But if your risk management is a little off, it will insure that you will never be able to tell a good entry from a bad one.

The hope is that these charts will make my point clear enough. Focus on that tiny part of the graph on the left. You must, you must, you must fit into that tiny section if you ever hope to be successful as a trader. But we are not yet finished. In this chapter we have seen very clearly how the novice goes broke. It's not difficult and can be done over a long period of time and very consistently. But in the next chapter we will show you how treacherous that little section on the left side of the graph can be. The trader must fully understand what the future holds. Otherwise it will be impossible to stay the course when the going gets rough. And it will.

---

[62] The mistake that underlies the thesis of this paragraph is that there is a limited amount of wealth in the world to go around, i.e., it's a zero sum game. Try to remember—anything that is generally accepted by the crowd is worth reconsidering. This one is the biggest mistake to ever come down the pike. It is the title to another book. Here's the summary—most, if not all, of the wealth in America did not exist when we arrived.

FYX

First let us struggle with our "Christian disadvantage." Then we'll deal with scriptural percentages.

None of my readers, even you Christians, will appreciate the disadvantage that we Christians have when it comes to the theme of this chapter. Every religion has some feature of God that they emphasize. For a Hindu, God is every *thing*. For Islam, God is merciful. For the Jew, G-d is one—and so holy we dare not spell his name. For us Christians, God is sovereign. That is fundamental to being a Christian. If you don't think God is sovereign, you may not be a Christian. God knows all. He created the universe knowing all that would happen. That is why he gets blamed for the problem of evil; he caused it, even if only is some remote way.[63] I will spare you a discussion of that here except as it applies to us traders. It applies to us because with a sovereign hanging out in the universe, there is no such thing as luck.[64] And therefore the law of averages is suspect, and probably[65] does not apply to us Christians.

Granted that this is an over-simplified summary of the problem. So let me cut the theory and hurry to a very real example: You have never heard a pastor or theologian explain why David picked up those other four stones. Remember? At

---

[63] You surely know about the problem of evil—if God had not said, "Bang," or "Let there be light," (depending on your translation), there would not be evil because there would not be a world. So he gets the blame (or credit). But I dare not get sidetracked on this problem. Nevertheless, I offer a suggestion for your consideration. From personal experience, I know that ninety percent (or more) of all the thinking that gets done on a baseball field is done by the catcher. And the Hall of Fame catcher-philosopher of the Yankees, Yogi Berra, solved the problem of evil when he said, "It's never over 'till it's over." (See chapter six for a little more on this topic—not Yogi, the other.)

[64] Have you heard a Christian artist sing, "Have Yourself a Merry Little Christmas?" They cannot bear to sing that last part, "Through the years we all will be together, if the fates allow." So they sing, "If the Lord allows." They illustrate my point: Christians do not believe in luck. You will be intrigued to research the evolution of the lyrics of the song.

[65] Many a theologian will object to my use of the word "probably" here. To them it is a certainty that luck does not exist.

the brook before facing the giant? Let us suppose you have heard about Goliath having four brothers. Fine. That is a joke. It is a fair generalization that theologians do not emphasize their sense of humor until they need a distraction from the issues they would like to avoid.

Here's their problem: Why would a great hero of the faith, who trusted God implicitly, ever waste his time and add to his load by picking up four extra rocks? I'll soon be accused of heresy, but the fact is that even these great heroes of the faith were practical, down-to-earth people who had a thorough understanding of the law of averages. He knew full well that he would be presumptive to take only one rock, not to mention the embarrassment of having to retreat to the brook in the middle of a fight for more ammo.

David had enough confidence in God's grace that he tells the giant what he will do with his head, and other stuff—this was history's first recording of trash talking. If a hero of such great faith has to respect the law of averages, you and I will have to do the same.

And because the law of averages is all about percentages, let us turn to that theme, a topic on which the scripture is well versed. Jesus surprised them with his emphasis on percentage when he honored the lady with the two mites. The value of her gift was a matter of percentage.[66]

Job doubled up on his wealth in the end.[67]

The parable of the talents deals with percentages, even though they are a bit extreme—1000, 500, 100 and zero percent returns.[68] I know you don't believe me because you've never heard your pastor put it in those terms. But I am simply quoting Jesus. These numbers were not real, you understand. He made them up. It was a parable, a product of his imagination. But does this not show how important these numbers are if he would

---

[66] Lk 21:4; Mk 12:43

[67] Job 42: 10 You never hear about Job being a greedy guy. Why not? Surely the man knew something about maximizing his profits.

[68] Mt 25:14f, Lk 19:12f

make up the numbers to highlight his story? Further, I submit, the numbers are realistic.[69]

Sapphira and her spouse said 100 percent when some smaller percent would have been more accurate.[70] What were they thinking? That was so unnecessary. Can we assume that they got buried together? We are spiritually dozing off by supposing that God is not serious about our cash, and the percentages we use to represent it.

Most curious of all the percentages of scripture was Jesus' request that the Rich Young Ruler liquidate 100 percent.[71] And a very short time later, maybe even the next day, Zacchaeus offered 50 percent.[72] The man doesn't have the common decency to put a specific number of talents on his gift. Who can forget that amazing story? And Jesus supported his approach, saying, "Today salvation has come to this house." There is hardly an evangelical theologian today who would concur with such a statement of faith. Can't you hear them correcting him? "Zacchaeus, you can't buy your way into the kingdom. It's not about money; it's about faith, and having Jesus in your heart." (That settles it—I am anathema now. Thus endeth my hope for an endorsement from an evangelical pastor.)

The more they say that it's not about money, the more you can be sure that it is about money. If you gave someone a raw deal, forget the apology and write a check.

Let me conclude this chapter with the point on which the scripture agrees with me unequivocally.[73] The human desire to get

---

[69] Matthew and Luke record two separate parables. The themes are similar, but the numbers are in sharp contrast. To get you curious, consider that Matthew's story uses talanta (which has, quite properly, become our word for "gifted"), a measure of gold which is approximately 60 times more valuable than Luke's word, mina. (All of the stories of Jesus are amazing, as these two will demonstrate.)

[70] Acts 5:1f

[71] Matt 19:16f; Mk 10:17f; Lk 18:18f

[72] Lk 19:2f, Zach is only in Luke

[73] My prayer is that you will begin to see a pattern—my desire to have all my ideas supported by holy writ. This one just happens to be so important, so ignored, and so obvious to even a casual observer.

rich quick is a thinly veiled violation of the last commandment, the prohibition against covetousness. This is certainly the most underrated of all the commandments. We return to the Proverbs for details. "Dishonest money dwindles away, but he who gathers money little by little makes it grow."[74] That is the ultimate, "get rich slowly," mandate.

"A faithful man will abound with blessings, but whoever hastens to be rich will not go unpunished."[75]

And the mother lode of proof: "A stingy man hurries after riches, and doesn't know that poverty waits for him."[76]

It may be that all we have achieved in this chapter is to put the wisdom of Proverbs into a formula that proves the peril of ignoring that amazing book. And if you don't know the power of the word peril, you have not yet traded.

---

[74] Proverbs 13:11, NIV
[75] Proverbs 28:20, English Standard Version
[76] Proverbs 28:22, English Standard Version

CHAPTER FIVE

HOW BAD CAN IT BE?

In the last chapter we learned how easily we can lose in this business. We saw that anyone on the right side of that graph is good for 100 trades or so, and then off into some other line of work. And they did this with a statically guaranteed winning system. They gave it a shot, are gone, and wishing they had listened to many of us who begged them to stay away in the first place. Fine.

For those of you who were not serious enough to commit to a number in that game, you are wasting your time. I'm puzzled that you are still reading. You're not a trader. You might be an academic—get another book and find an ivory tower.[77] And fear not—many a brainstorm had its origin in the tower.

Now let us have a look at what life will be like for the rest of us—those who are chicken enough to trade so conservatively that we never leave the left side of that graph.

---

[77] If you are tiring of this line, bear with me, please. You see, if this effort is successful, a number of trader wannabes will see the light and avoid our industry. If you are among them, it will save you a fortune in time, stress, and capital. But more importantly, it will free you to achieve something significant in some other line of work.

For you pro traders, here is the formula on which the RR is based:

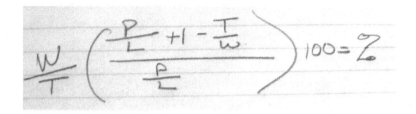

$$\frac{W}{T}\left(\frac{\frac{P}{L}+1-\frac{T}{W}}{\frac{P}{L}}\right)100 = Z$$

W—Total number of wins
T—Total number of trades
P—Size of average win
L—Size of average loss

When I first developed this concept, for the purpose of instilling the fear of God into a group of novice investors, these numbers were quite theoretical, almost ivory tower-like. But they must be taken out of the tower and put into practice. I have never started trading an idea without running it through this formula. Never.

To the left, you can see the numbers that we have been using on the RR to generate all the profit graphs in the previous chapter and this one as well. We have varied the percent to invest at the bottom. We used 50 and 20 in the last chapter. And in this chapter we will use 8 exclusively. It will achieve our goal, the maximizing of profit.

RITCHIERULE

Start Up Capital
i 100

Win/Loss %   Win Count
i 50   Loss Count   *i*

Average Win   Average Loss
i 12   10   *i*

Investment [TO RISK ON EACH TRADE]
Dollars   8.00   *i*
Percentage   8   *i*

Invest 10   Times

Below you can see the same formula with these numbers plugged in:

W (total number of wins)–1
T (total number of trades)–2
P (average profit)–12 *(The RR will not do 1.2 so we use 10 & 12)*
L (average loss)—10

$$\frac{1}{2}\left(\frac{\frac{1.2}{1}+1-\frac{2}{1}}{\frac{1.2}{1}}\right)100 = 8\frac{1}{3}\%$$

It will not give you any pain to spend a moment analyzing this formula.[78] The formula tells us that 8 1/3 is the optimum percent to invest. This will maximize our profits and keep us in business as we reduce trading size during drawdowns.[79]

After developing and using this formula for about twenty years, I ran into a friend from outside the business who wanted to learn to trade. He recognized the concept, dragged out a math text, and showed me that I was not the first to notice the phenomenon. It is now popularly known as the Kelly formula. I believe that Thorpe did some work on it as well. When I did my interview for the Market Wizard series, I didn't feel like getting into this much detail; I'd never read Kelly's math text, and all the seminars I ever attended never mentioned the issue. Therefore, let me hasten to give credit to Kelly and Thorpe.

What's more, I recall a conversation Thorpe was kind enough to have with me back in the sixties–about his blackjack theory which I had learned. Back then, directory assistance would

---

[78] You'll notice that you are inverting that winning percent and subtracting it. That means that if you win a third of the time and your wins are double your losses, that baby (numerator) is going to zero. A moment's reflection and you won't need a formula to tell you this.

[79] For the beginner, "drawdown" is our word for slump. Every trader has them. If you don't want to have a trading slump, get a job.

give you the phone number of almost any prof. (By the time you read this, who knows what the process of interpersonal contact will be.) And I do recall Thorpe saying, "Just keep your bet size small."

The comment was confusing because he appeared to have an unlimited amount of cash with which to experiment, not to mention wigs, mustaches, and a of other paraphernalia.[80]

By the time I began, and for thirty years after, I never heard or saw the formula. Indeed, when I shared this info in a seminar recently, no one there was aware of the formula or its value. So I said, "It may be that I'm not the first to develop the formula, but I am the first to tell you that you cannot trade without it."

Now we are set. We are ready and committed to stay way over on the left side of that crude, pencil-drawn graph. We are still using theoretical numbers, but they are winning numbers. And for our test experiment, we will use the optimum number, 8 percent.[81] So let us run the RR and see what life is going to be like now that we really know what we are doing. You are a born-again risk taker, turned so conservative you feel like a coward.

In the last chapter we started with $100. But let's be as realistic as possible. We'll use our 401k and call it $100,000. That way we can imagine this is a real trading scenario, not just a game.

Remember I told you that we would be paying off the national debt at the end of the second week. Forget the third week. Let's see what the starting trades might look like. The following charts will show the kind of returns that the law of averages might give you. I got this example on my second try using the RR.

---

[80] Get the book, *Beat the Dealer*. But don't try it. The market will be easier.

[81] Actually the optimum is 8 1/3, but we have learned our lesson—always err on the conservative side. Never fail to honor that yellow stripe.

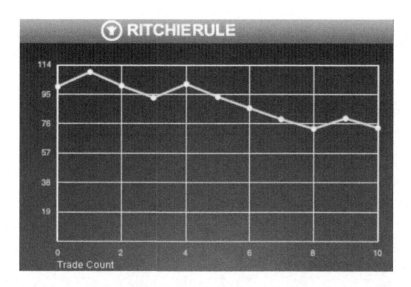

You can see that after 10 trades we are down about 25 percent. This is a bad drawdown, but we have confidence. We've had a bad run of luck. So we take heart and continue trading.

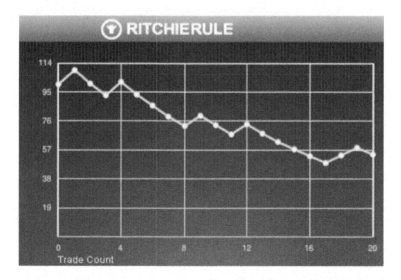

After the 20th trade we are beginning to lose faith in the law of averages. We may have some doubts about our entry and exit points. We're down about 45 percent and having huge doubts about this RR thing. We're thinking seriously about bailing out. But for some reason, we continue.

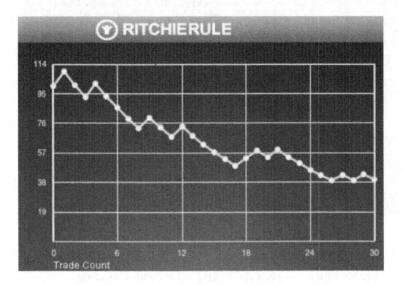

After 30 trades you can see we are down about 60 percent, the law of averages looks like an idiot, and we are looking for a gun with which to get whatever fool taught us about the RR. (We have forgotten what it stands for and Ritchie has gone into hiding)

Now the maxim for you to consider: Many of life's failures were people who did not realize how close they were to success before they gave up. (Here's another of those places to stop and think that over. We will revisit the theme for sure.) Every professional trader lives by this maxim.

You convince yourself that things can't get any worse—your most recent mistake—and you continue to allow the law of averages to pound you. So get a load of the 40-trade chart. Check out that horrible run of luck you had going up to trade number 38. Yikes. You are sucking air now. You review all your numbers and remind yourself that you set out to risk 100K so what difference will it make if you lose the last 35K.

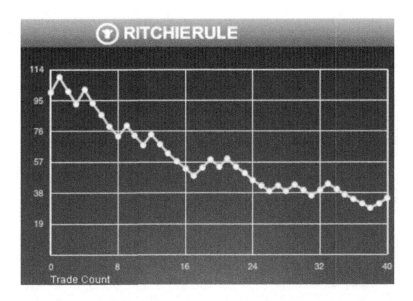

You are beginning to curse the RR and you might even give me a call. What can I tell you that I haven't already told you, what everybody told you from the beginning? Do not invest more than you are willing to lose. So if you are not willing to lose the last 35K, you fooled yourself in the beginning. Obviously you are savvy enough to never listen to those account executives who would ask if you'd like to trade your 100K as if it were 200K. They would have closed your account back around trade number 17 and told you they had done their best for you.

So you call me and I tell you, "What have you got to lose?"

You say, "35K."

I say, "Be sure to continue reducing your size so that you never over trade." You are not impressed.

Then to give you a little handholding encouragement, I remind you that many of life's failures were people who did not realize how close they were to success before they gave up. You tell me that you remember the line very well, but that I should have told you how painful and difficult it would be to continue. Then I give you my punch line. I tell you that I plagiarized the quote from Thomas Edison and I didn't credit him because I

93

needed you to concentrate on the quote, not the author; we all know we're not Thomas Edison. With that gravitas added to your trading style, you go back at it.

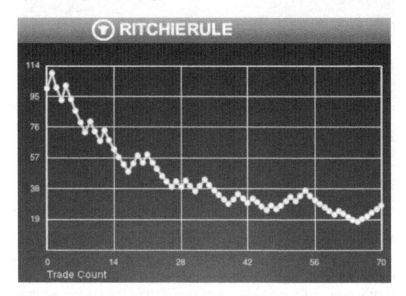

Sure enough, gravitas from Edison and assurance from Ritchie does nothing to save you from the law of averages. (He should have mentioned that it wouldn't–it's so obvious.) Things get worse. But cheer up. You do get a moment of reprieve between trade 65 and 70. There is not a sensible person in the world who would tell you to continue this trend. Just look at that graph. You are down 80 percent, a drawdown of biblical proportions, far more than you can stomach. Wanna quote Einstein again? About doing the same thing over and over?

No doubt some of you are wondering if the RR app is giving us an idea of how the *real* world works. These numbers are generated totally by the law of averages. Like I said, this group of numbers happened on the second time I ran this trading system. The scenario you are viewing is not rare. It could happen to any of us. So you close your eyes, bite the bullet (as we say so often), consider the last of your 401k lost, and continue.

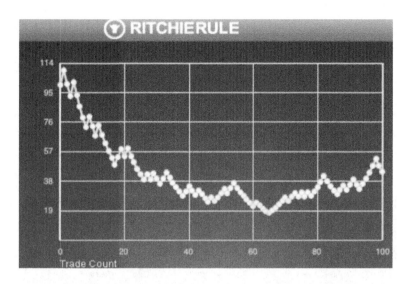

Now finally by trade 100 you have almost doubled your money from your worst drawdown. You surely will not stop now. All you need is stay in business and eventually lady luck will smile on you. You know this will require great patience, but you are learning that for sure. And you've got the most critical lesson: How to stay the course. Have a look at trade 65 and trade 119.

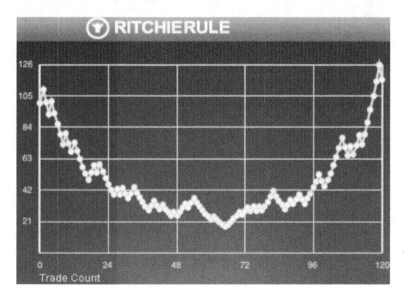

And what's more, let's check the win-loss record. You will see in the next graph, below, that you are slightly ahead in spite of a law of averages that has not been kind to you, only 58 wins from 120 trades. It would not have been possible for you to achieve this without adjusting your trading sizes as you have. And we have already observed that you would have come to the same total no matter what order the wins and losses had fallen.

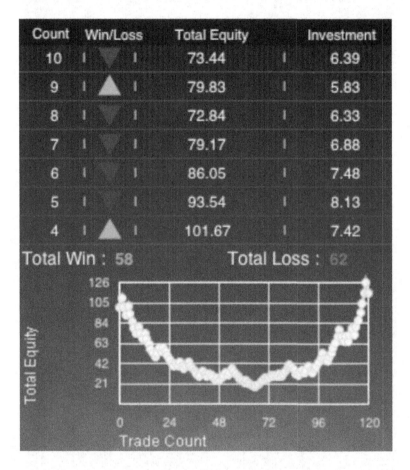

Count	Win/Loss	Total Equity		Investment
10	▼	73.44	ı	6.39
9	▲	79.83	ı	5.83
8	▼	72.84	ı	6.33
7	▼	79.17	ı	6.88
6	▼	86.05	ı	7.48
5		93.54	ı	8.13
4	▲	101.67	ı	7.42

Total Win : 58   Total Loss : 62

Now that you have seen how Ritchie's Rule can dig you out of a hole, you are ready to continue with disciplined abandon.

Good for you. We will take future ups and downs in stride from now on. So let's go straight to trade number 240.

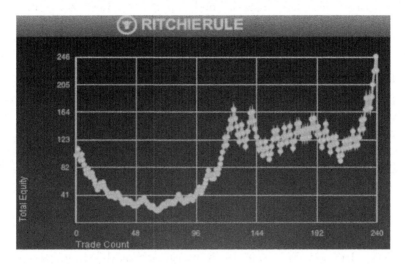

You can see that you got jerked around considerably between trade 120 and 220. But what is that among traders of your stature now? All you have to do is follow the rules, and sooner or later you get the run up. Here's the proof.

Okay, finally. You have arrived. Ritchie has proven himself at last. You are singing my praises. You are in demand at the cocktail parties. You are contemplating quitting your day job—if you haven't already. You are done quoting Einstein and now you quote Edison exclusively. There is no more holy grail talk. That was all theoretical. This is real and it's Holy Cow.

And your banker? She has rolled out the red carpet for you. What better proof does she need than you doubling your money, and more? It's time for that vacation home, the condo on the beach in Sanibel, the motorhome, and the rest of your heart's desire. To put it in my friend Larry Burkett's voice: "The wife buys five new dresses; and the husband buys a boat, a motorhome, and a Ferrari." The point is that you celebrate; and after that drawdown you traded through, you deserve a celebration. You and the whole family.

But one thing is certain: You do not take your money out of the market. You do nothing to so much as injure that golden goose, or even make it mad. There's no need to. Your banker will facilitate almost anything you desire once she sees your total equity and your trading record.

And the kids? Pepperdine, Boston College, and for the family genius, Notre Dame or Rutgers. No problem. The proof of the pudding is in the eating; you will develop clichés of your own for those cocktail parties. You have followed sound advice. You are a proven success. You won't stop now until you reach your first million. Let me be the first to welcome you to the ranks of professional traders. Naturally, like any pro, you do all this purchasing quietly. You want to avoid that "smartest-guy-in-the-room" image.

There is nothing wrong with this thinking. You have turned $100K into $250K. What more proof do you need? Okay, let's continue trading. Remember that this is just one sample of what *might* happen. I remind you that this one happened on my second try; it is no outlier.

Have a look at our next chart.

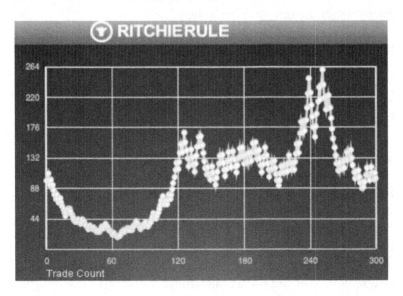

Not to worry, you are an experienced trader now. We know that these drawdowns happen to the best of them even though we are about down to where we started, $100K. Let us continue. And we will hope that lady luck does not test us like she did before.

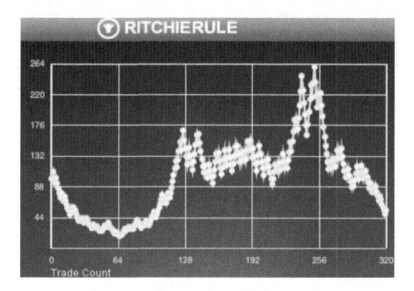

Most of us have outgrown our nightmare stage—too bad for you—because you're having one now. And that is only assuming that you can get to sleep.

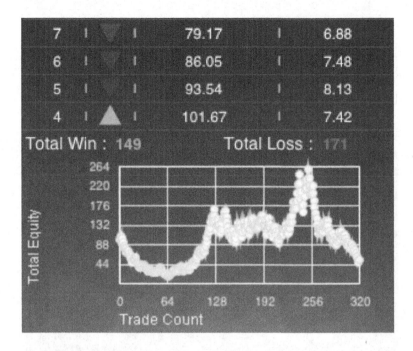

7	▼	79.17	6.88
6	▼	86.05	7.48
5	▼	93.54	8.13
4	▲	101.67	7.42

Total Win : 149   Total Loss : 171

You check the actual TE to see if this is possible. Sure enough, there's your account at trade 7[82] with $79,170 left in it, about $21,000 less than what you started with 320 trades ago.

Now the bad news, I mean the really bad news: This drawdown is *nothing* like the previous. Now you have infused yourself with confidence that you never had before. You have not needed to spend any money to do all the things you dreamed about doing. And you've got huge payments on all those dreams. Your payments have been sucking money out of your account almost as fast as this drawdown has. And the kids? They are off at Notre Dame or Boston College, $50,000 a year at either place, while the motorhome and boat payments get withdrawn automatically. You surely have not paid cash for anything because your capital is being put to such good use.

---

[82] It shows up on this chart as trade number 7 because I have been doing this "trading" ten trades at a time in order to watch this event unfold. Actually we crossed below $80K at approximately trade number 300.

Your spouse cannot understand why your fuse is shorter than normal, you are distracted, and no fun anymore.

Go ahead and get yourself a good laugh now. Because when this happens to you, there will be no joy in Mudville. Remember that pastor I told you about? When I mentioned suicide, he knew that I knew what he was going through. The title of chapter one is neither joke nor flippant.

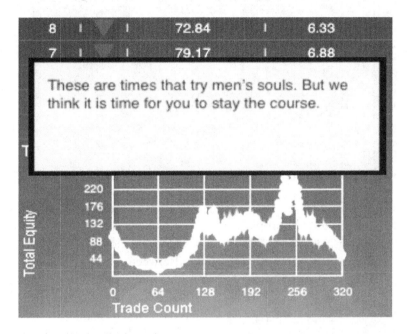

Then some smart-ass creator of the RR has the gall to put up a comment like the one on this graph. "Easy for them to say," you think to yourself. You wouldn't normally use the phrase *smart ass*. But have no fear, no one will blame you for expanding your vocabulary at a time like this.

The important thing is to never say that it cannot get any worse. We will discuss the existence of God in the next chapter. But for now, there is nothing that stirs God to action like anyone saying what cannot happen. I admit that this concept could be the knee jerk reaction from a guy who is suspicious of what God is up to. So forget the theology and focus on the law of averages—things can always get worse.

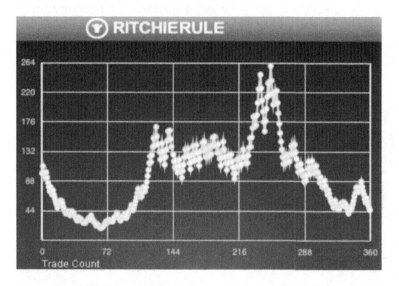

In this case they get better for a little, but by trade 360 you are back down in the dumps.

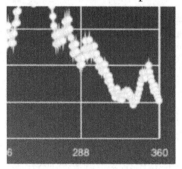

Here's a closer look if you like. Between 340 and 360 you have a run up to almost the $100K where you started. But then back down again.

It will be no stretch to assume that by trade 360 you are busted. You can no longer meet your margin calls. You have made a classic mistake. You did not take *any* money off the table. You continued to risk it all. You got too confident. Indeed, you did take money off the table when you incurred the debt. My friend, Burkett, spent his entire career telling anyone who would listen, not to do this. Some listened, not many. But you are unique; you deceived yourself by thinking that you had cash in your account to back up every dollar you borrowed. So the money was not literally taken off the table. But each loan was a contingent liability that strained your trading account. So depending on your spending habits during that huge increase in your equity, you are likely broke at this time and unable to make your margin calls. Resale on motorhomes is terrible. Boats are worse. And those margin calls don't give you a lot of time. But in case you are not broke at this point, let's see what the law of averages might do to you in the next hundred trades.

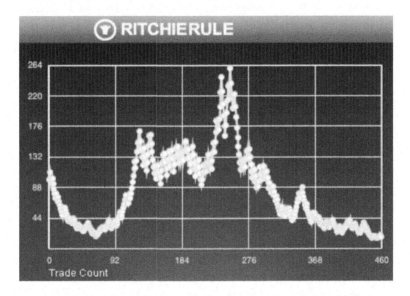

That should just about wrap it up. I sure hope you have at least paid up that Boston College tuition and room and board. That way you can break the news to your kid when she gets home and has to work all summer in order to pay for community college. The Boston College credits will transfer there, no problem. But the talk around campus is going to be brutal. She might be a sweetie, but don't expect her to be happy.

You have no choice but to stop your trading and begin to liquidate your holdings in an attempt to regroup and get back in the market. Such an idea would be supported by any prudent person.

While you are regrouping, let us consider how you got yourself into a drawdown that was so large you had to stop trading your system? You started out at the optimum level and then you slipped very easily into over-trading. That was so easy to miss. We could use the word greed if we wanted. But this is a difficult and personal issue, and for our purposes, we don't need to go there. However, it is a matter that I will leave to you with the message that it cannot be ignored.

While I leave you to contemplate the role of greed, let me introduce another problem. You did not anticipate the kind of drawdown that the law of averages can give you. Go ahead, call her lady luck if you like; but it is really a law. This law has the ability to deal you a blow so ugly that it will almost always be mistaken for a change in market conditions. This will put you out of business, not because the market threw you a curve you couldn't hit, but because you failed to anticipate what the law of averages could do to you.

Please take this to heart: You must play around with the RR enough that you become comfortable with what the law of averages can do to any system you might initiate. Without this comfort level, you are doomed to over-analysis, second-guessing, twenty-twenty hindsight, reoptimization, and other items of distraction that you will create on your own.

Don't make the mistake of thinking that an app with a price of 99 cents can't be worth much. The best advice one often gets is free. That's why they call them parents. You must have a good idea of what that law can do to you. That way you can adjust your trading size to accommodate it.

The alternative will be ugly, as you are about to see. Because now we are going to look ahead at your trading system to see what would have happened if we had kept trading during the time that you are out of the market and regrouping.

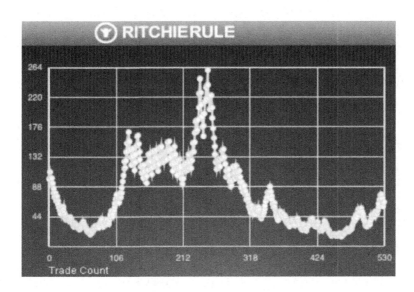

You can see that by trade 530 you would have been on your way toward break-even.

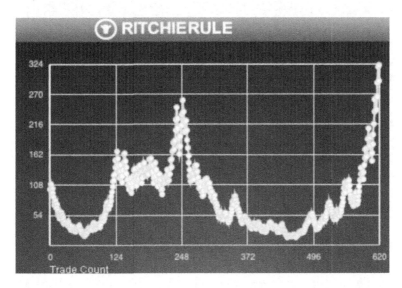

The winning continues until at trade 620 you are making new equity highs (over $300,000). I am completely at loss to explain it, but the good and the bad do seem to come in bunches.

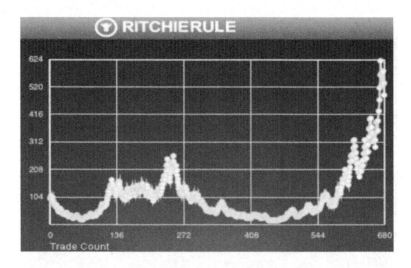

At trade 680 you have passed the $600,000 mark.

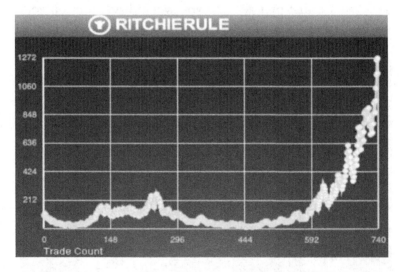

Here is trade 740 and you would have passed the million-dollar mark at 1 1/4 mil. It is against the law in our business to say *I told you so*. But it isn't recommended. Anyone who looks back at a trader's record and suggests what they should have done is waving the flag of trading imbecility.[83] With that disclaimer, you will surely recall that I said this system was a winner. Here's more of what happened while you were selling the motor home:

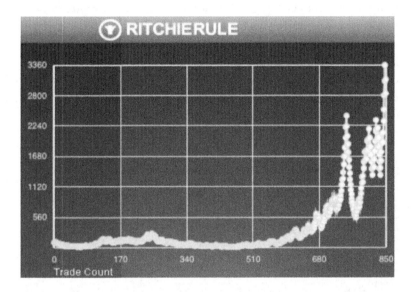

At trade 850 you would have made new equity highs passing the 3-mil mark. Of course you cannot escape noticing the pain of that drawdown back to half a mil. You can rejoice that you missed that.

Nevertheless, the real problem is that you are missing *all* this stuff, and we're looking back just to see how things might have gone had we been able to continue trading. Every trader will gain satisfaction with my writing if I can get you to appreciate our favorite phrase—woulda-coulda-shoulda. Maybe we

---

[83] I had a professional recently look back at a trade I made in the 70s and characterize it as stupid. That's when it dawned on me why this trader has struggled over the years, never succeeding enough to buy a seat on any exchange. A real trader uses hindsight on his own trades, never on a someone else's trade. But he has done pretty well analyzing the errors of others, in that case mine. His articles are widely published. He even wrote a book.

ought to review that Thomas Edison quote, or would that be too painful?

By the time we get over 1,100 trades under your belt, that problem at trade 800 looks like a minor hiccup. You can see that we are still getting great volatility, but at 28 mil one would think we could suffer with a little volatility. But that is a typical line coming from the mouth of the novice. Anyone can speculate what sort of volatility they might be able to withstand with quantities of money they don't have. We have proven that we cannot take the volatility of 6 figures ($100K to $250K). How can we guess what we might do with 8 figures?

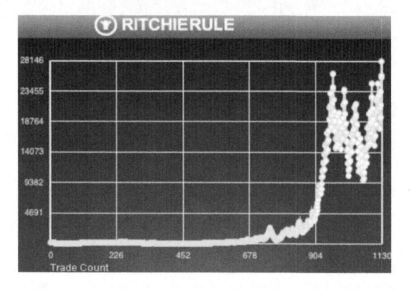

During the next 60 trades, up to trade 1190, we would have had a terrific run of luck—28 mil up to 86 mil.

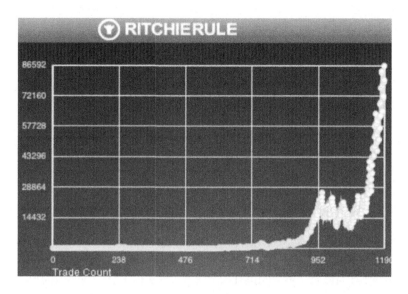

That is enough. We've made our point, which is that the theoretical winnings shown here and in the next graph look pretty innocuous–a very simple run from 100K up to 92 billion. It looks smooth, but in fact it may be a path that no human being could follow.

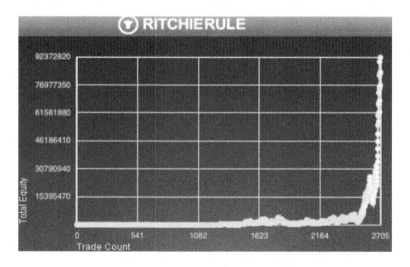

Okay—you have just had an introduction to hell—or some sort of advance glimpse at it. So you made a billion? Big deal. It will not feel like it was worth it. I read this chapter to Nancy. When I got to the part where the kids came home from Boston College for summer break, she could take no more. She begged me to stop reading.

Now remember, we used the optimal number, 8 percent. Anything higher than that would have been worse, far worse. Anything higher than 16 2/3 would have guaranteed failure. But we found a way to fail with the optimum number. Who could have survived all those drawdowns? As this purely random series turned out, almost any trader would have been forced out of the market in the wake of the drawdown from 250K to 20K. And don't think that the storyboard I fictionalized to accompany this is unrealistic in the slightest. Edison's line is a prophetic nightmare. This is no life for you. It is no life for anyone.

Twenty years ago, when Schwager asked about money management, I said a half of a percent of total equity. A typical trader, if there is one, might say between one to two percent, and that would vary widely depending on the confidence in the situation. I recall a trader commenting on an opportunity by referring to it as the trade on which to mortgage the house and anything else available. But these percentages are merely a fraction of the story, literally.

Here are the numbers: At the time of the Wizards interview, I might have been executing about two hundred strategies. If one assigned $10,000 to each of them, and had a system that called for twenty percent to be invested on each trade, that would allow $2,000 to be risked on any single trade, meaning $2,000 from each entry point to the stop-loss for that entry point.[84] But 20 percent split among 200 systems (more accurately, "divided by") gives the trader one tenth of one percent of total capital on each trade. That is a mere fraction of the one to two percent commonly mentioned. And BTW, no doubt you

---

[84] If it's 20 tics from entry point to the stop and $10 per tic, you put on 10 contracts, making a total loss of $2,000.

noticed that there is quite a difference between one percent and two percent. So you see, when I said that my answer to Schwager was a fraction of the story, literally, I was using that word, "literally," the way we baby-boomers use it—remember that dictionary definition?

The point: No pro trader would ever risk 20 percent of his capital on anything, certainly not a trade. And it's hard for me to imagine two percent either. Sound boring does it? Good. More to come on the topic of boring.

A MORE PRACTICAL REALITY

In the last chapter we were a guaranteed failure. In this chapter we got math on our side, the law of averages with us, traded the optimum numbers, and still we failed. If you are getting that sinking feeling in the pit of your stomach, you are beginning to get this business figured out. Is there any hope?

Let me present three alternatives which may be workable. Take whichever one fits your personality. You might first review that number you wrote on the page in the last chapter. Is your reality undergoing some adjustments? Good.

First:	Typical Pro Trader
Second:	Brandt-Thorpe Modification
Third:	My Modification

FIRST: TYPICAL PRO TRADER

A typical trader[85] will select a number arbitrarily and use it for the worst loss. Typically this number will be between one tenth of one percent and two percent of total capital. This is why almost no professional trader uses this formula and will surely be suspicious of my 8 percent number. Do not for one second

---

[85] There is no such thing as a typical trader. I've made that point. This industry has room for a wide variety of trading styles and personality types. We are hoping you can find yours. But this "Typical Pro Trader" is my best guess at the most common approach to this problem.

overlook how far we have moved toward the conservative side from where we began in chapter four.

One day I met a trader in the pit who was making the mistake I've been outlining in this and the previous chapter. He was relatively new and we talked a little bit about his trading style. We actually had the same spread on. We knew it was a good position but he was nervous.[86] He told me how much he had on and I told him that was too much. The next morning when we met he told me how right I was and thanked me for the tip. Obviously he had not slept well. He said, "I'm cutting my position in half at the opening this morning." Okay, I thought, fine. But in actual fact, I suspected that cutting his position in half would not get him into the ballpark of where he should be. I was guessing that he needed to cut it by at least 90 percent, probably more.

He's out of trading today, but is an excellent analyst, and many traders buy his market analysis and use it to make money trading. Because I never scrutinized his personal finances, I cannot be totally certain, but I suspect that the difference between success and failure for this trader was simply a matter of trading size.

I have said it often; now you may begin to see it: "We traders have a yellow streak running down our backs that would shock the public." They think we are wild gamblers. That yellow streak is what keeps us profitable over the years. A typical pro will make up a conservative number, say half a percent of total equity, and will risk that amount on every trade until they are convinced that their entry and exit points have failed them or proven profitable.

SECOND: BRANDT-THORPE MODIFICATION

Cut your percent to invest by half and you will cut your losses in half and reduce your profit margin by 25 percent. Any time you can cut your risk in half and only hurt your profit by a

---

[86] Traders don't normally swap personal information about their trading strategies. Market analysis, on the other hand, is cheap and flows like water.

quarter, do it. That is, as we say in the business, a no-brainer. You can quote me on that and make it a battle cry if you like. There's that yellow streak again.

If you look back at that hand-drawn graph, you will recall that using our optimum 8 percent, we made $.83 after two trades. If we use this modification and only invest 4 percent, we will have $.61 after two trades. Run the numbers for yourself; you might as well get used to running these numbers. You can see that while you have obviously reduced your risk by half,[87] you have only reduced your profit by a quarter.[88] No trader will pass up that bargain.

Thorpe made this observation some decades back and I credit Brandt with it as well because a trader with his experience has surely put this to the test in the real world. After the erratic profits you've been looking at, one cannot argue with decades of success. Brandt and I crossed paths back in the 70's on the floor. We have no specific recollection of yelling at each other, but the law of averages would strongly favor it.

You may recall from chapter two that it was this very trader, Peter Brandt, who discouraged me from writing this book. That is what legitimate traders do; they discourage anything that will hurt the investor. And Brandt assumed that any book that encourages people to trade is leading them astray. The problem is that there is no financial reward for giving such sound advice. This is why you and the public in general are constantly bombarded with alternate messages–"Buy gold. Buy silver," and on and on.

---

[87] If you have $10K committed to a system, your stop will be $400 away instead of $800.

[88] These numbers (83 and 61) don't come out exactly at 75 percent. This is because we have not used the precise numbers, which would be 8 1/3 and 4 1/6. If you ran those numbers, the lower (4 1/6) should produce 75 percent of the higher (8 1/3).

THIRD: MY MODIFICATION

Diversify.

First the harsh warning: Why did the incredibly talented, even brilliant, doctor end up with a stud racehorse that turned out to be a gelding? (And a doctor, mind you.) Why does the commodities trader get involved in limited partnerships? Why do I buy gas and oil wells? We do this because we have fallen into the diversification trap. So we get involved in areas of our greatest ignorance.[89] If you are a trader or an investor, you can get all the diversification that anyone could ever want. Our business is amply stacked with pitfalls and shortcomings, but lack of diversification is not one of them. If you own Apple, Walmart, and ADM stock, anyone who tells you that you need more diversification needs to have their head diversified.

Now my modification: You will need a broad diversification of trading ideas. Suppose you have ten systems, all of which require 8 percent. Now you are risking 8/10 of a percent on each trade. And your equity curve will smooth out. If you have a 100K account and 10K allotted to each system, then each trade will risk $800. Thus I would not be afraid to invest 8 percent of my widely divided capital in such a system as long as I had confidence that it was not over-optimized. (More to come on that problem.) At about 50 systems you will begin to achieve the kind of smooth equity curve you can be successful with over time.

EVALUATION

The Typical Pro Trader approach is, first of all, purely a guess on my part. No one knows exactly each trader's approach. But

---

[89] And we invariably do this with a character we do not know well enough. We take someone else's "recommendation" on a third party's skill and integrity. This constitutes the introduction to another book which I refuse to write. I once received a check (6 figures) from an associate to cover the losses I incurred from the dishonest person whose talent he had recommended. My point, and do not miss it: We are now in a new millennium; that level of integrity is no longer available to you or to me.

it should also be noted that it is a guess on their part too. They have no objective way to know what size to invest. It is generally done by the seat of the pants. They are good at it. So I would NEVER tell a successful trader to change a proven system. If you are a pro, stick with what got you here.

Strength: It is conservative enough to keep one from going broke by overtrading.

Weakness: 1) It doesn't come close to maximizing profits. 2) It does not require a system to come back from a drawdown by trading smaller.

The Brandt-Thorpe Modification is especially to be recommended if you do not have confidence in your entry points. It will take great stress off a system that is being newly initiated. However, it still lacks diversity.

My modification will give you the maximum bang per dollar of capital. You will get no objection from me for starting every system with the Brandt modification. If you get your sizing right and don't overlook the over-optimization problem, you can require your systems to recover their losses by trading smaller. That way a system can fade away and die a natural and quiet death.

AFTERTHOUGHTS

WORST LOSSES

Your stop must be the distance away from your entry point so as to replicate your *worst* loss, *not* your average loss. If your worst loss is five times the size of your average loss, you will find you are committing far more capital than you had originally planned. This will throw all calculations off considerably–or make you far more conservative than you first thought. Do your best to correct this problem by developing systems that have as consistent losses as possible. If you have a $1,000 stop, your average loss might be $800. Good. But if you carry positions overnight, look out. You have greatly increased your risk. And if you carry positions over the weekend, look out more. Now you have exponentially increased your risk. Please recall that we have generally been talking short term trading. This does not mean that you cannot carry over the weekend. You can. But you must understand the risk. That means you must have capital set aside to offset that risk.[90]

OVER-OPTIMIZATION (The bane of our industry)

Any computer can survey past data and curve fit a system that would have[91] made a fortune. The computer has better hindsight than any of us. There is no advice in this book or any other that is able to overcome an over-optimized, curve fitted, back-tested system. That boilerplate cliché, "Past performance is no guarantee of future results," is not to be ignored. Even a real track record can be over-optimized. It happens every day. Here's how:

Suppose you, the client, say to your investment advisor, "Can you show me the real trades on a real account?" The investment advisor goes to his filing cabinet. He has one thousand accounts from which to pick. Do you suppose he will show you a losing account? Does he show you his "average" account? No. He "curve fits" the accounts he shows you. And a year later you wonder why you weren't quite as "lucky" as all those clients with the real track records that were so profitable. They were real. They were just curve fitted.

I still cannot believe that I allowed myself to become involved with a group that had a marvelously back-tested system with which they had never traded. So it might come as no surprise to learn that some, if not all, of the principals had served time, are serving time, may yet serve time, or have disappeared in order to avoid that fate.

Many topics in this book are merely introduced. This one, for example. You will have to work this out on your

---

[90] Just paint that yellow streak down your back a little wider.

[91] Whenever you hear that phrase, "would have," you must look deeper behind the sentence in which it is used. Same goes for "could have," and "should have."

own. Presumably you can see the problem. You can feed the computer one concept after another, adjust it with filters to catch those problem trades, overload it with parameters, and you are guaranteed to come up with something, something that would have worked if you had known all those parameters in advance. And there's that *would have* phrase again. Remember: When you hear that phrase, there is very likely a trap nearby.

Sure it would have worked, this back-tested group of ideas. Let us see if I can explain the pernicious nature of such a discovery. It makes you think you have found something when in fact all you have is a number-crunching computer with 20-20 hindsight. Pernicious is a very gentle word to use for this dangerous behavior. Your great-looking system might be nothing more than a highly complex woulda-coulda-shoulda that took a computer to discover.

Here are two suggestions that will help you get started in this effort.

First: It is a fair generalization to say that the more filters and parameters one needs to doctor a system, the more likely it is that the system is over-optimized.

Second: Beware of letting the computer do your thinking. The computer computes. You think. Translation: Your technical system, loaded with all your filters and optimized parameters, could be lacking in one fundamental[92] reason why it works. If you cannot so much as dream up one reason why your system has a fundamental basis in reality, it is likely over-optimized.

Early in my career I heard Jack Schwager address this problem in a seminar Q & A. He said not to run those massive optimizations in which the computer surveys every possible

---

[92] For you beginners: We have fundamentalists and technicians in our industry—just like ranchers and farmers of yesteryears. Fundamentalists love the fundamental factors, supply, demand and everything that affects those. Technicians bring order out of randomness (that's what we think, anyway). Techies say, "It's been up three days in a row, odds are it will be up tomorrow; therefore, buy." I can tell you that every pro trader will be curious that we are coming to the close of chapter 5 without this topic yet coming up. (I share that curiosity.) And even now it gets buried into a footnote.

parameter. Naturally the person asking the question wanted to know where he got his rules and parameters. Schwager shrugged a little and said, "Well, this is going to surprise you, but I just make them up." I'm still laughing as I recall that.

You will remember my assertion a few chapters back that this business is personality driven. I surely do not do what Schwager does; but neither do I argue with success. If it's working for you in real trading, don't let my theory talk you out of it.

You know by now that the thesis of this book is that people lose at investing because they trade too large. But it is also true that there is no more surefire way to develop a losing system than to over-optimize it.

The avoidance of over-optimization is an art. Be aware of it. Look for it. Avoid it.

FYX

This is too easy. James 5:1f speaks directly to the rich with a warning of the peril in store for them. And surely no Christian needs me to remind them of the warning of our Lord about the degree of difficulty for a rich person to enter the kingdom. He went so far as to emphasize the point with a revolting metaphor about a camel. I might as well be the first to admit that in my own struggle to maximize my profits, I have not taken that warning as seriously as the messenger did. This has been an easy mistake for me and all my millionaire Christian brothers to make. We have been misled in this mistake by our own clergy who have emphasized the attitude of the heart far ahead of what we actually do with our money. I will admit that I once heard a clergyman try to offset this mistake by specifying the model of car and the watch that a Christian should not own. (More to come on this for sure.)

But these themes—James, Jesus, and the camel—are a little bit ahead of us. These address the struggle of being wealthy. And in fact we are still in the throes of trying to give ourselves that problem. Who can forget Tevye's response to that semi-educated kid who called wealth a curse? "May the Lord smite me with it," he said. "And may I never recover." This is where we are. And we are now reviewing the bumpy road to achieving this "curse."

Therefore, the scriptural mandate that applies to us at this juncture is to get rich slowly. (Prov. 28:20) In case you didn't get enough on this topic from the last chapter, here we go again. Indeed, you have noticed by now that I seem to be in disagreement with a vast number of members of the cloth at many points in the book. This trend will continue. However, I'm not anti-clergy. They simply do not understand our industry. They are not alone.

Nevertheless, at this most critical point, we traders cross paths with the clergy and are in agreement with them one hundred percent. And we will not be shy about giving them all the credit due. The point of agreement will be so short lived that it will never get me off the heresy charge.

Here's the agreement: When you hear pulpiteers preach against our industry, they are really preaching against greed. But these past two chapters have been demonstrating mathematically the inherent danger of greed. If you would be successful, you must be able to lay greed aside. If greed is attracting you to our industry, listen to your pastor and get out. They get their wisdom from Proverbs and they are right. I use my formulas to show that the author of Proverbs knew whereof he spoke when he said to gain wealth slowly.

Here's one to make you wonder if the author of Proverbs was a comedian:

If you make your eyes rush at it, it's no longer there! For wealth will surely grow wings, like an eagle flying off to the sky.[93]

Do you get the feeling that whoever wrote that saw chapter four and five in advance? Hence the horns of the dilemma on which we sit. We have two goals: Avoid greed. Maximize profits.

An associate once asked me and my partner, "Is everything always profit with you guys?" Our attitude is pretty simple, "Do you want to stay in business?" If you struggle with the conflict between greed and maximizing profits, good for you. Keep it up.

And there is no better book in that regard than Proverbs. Any Christian worth their salt will read this book at regular intervals.[94] Make up your own length of time between readings.

---

[93] Prov. 23:5 CJB. BTW—I must mention the contribution my Jewish friends have made to my life. Humor. They told me about the synagogue that was being destroyed in a pogrom. The plunderers said, "We'll let everyone go, but execute the rabbi, the cantor, and the president of the synagogue." So they said to the three, "We will grant you each one last request before we shoot you." The rabbi says, "I will preach one last time." The cantor says, "I will sing one last time." The president of the synagogue says, "Shoot me first." Such humor can only be a gift from God.

[94] There are 31 chapters. Today is the 10th of August. I will read chapter 10.

We have already called your attention to Proverbs' emphasis on wisdom and discipline. Now let us add the word diligence. (Prov. 4:23; 10:4; 13:4; 21:5 and a whole lot more)

This is an easy matter to recognize. We've referred to it in the past and are repeating it here. If you are bored with your trading, you are on the right track. If you are hyped with adrenaline, you are catering to all the factors that will bring you down.

Elsewhere I have mentioned the popular preacher who mocked our business in general and Yuppies in particular with the claim that it was boring. I do not know of a place in holy writ, or any other religious writings, where boredom is used to measure value; I have struggled with moments of intense boredom when writing this material. (Go ahead, insert your own smart remarks here about the boredom you suffer reading it.)[95]

I would like my Christian brother, the preacher, to consider that one man's boredom is another man's diligence. Richard Dennis made this point when he said that the one time you fail to execute on a turn-around will be the time the trend starts and never looks back. Do not try to copy Dennis without developing diligence. He didn't call his students "turtles" for no reason. And get ready to deal with boredom even if that means closing your ears to certain preachers.

Boredom was the word I used with Schwager in his Market Wizards series. If you can't stand boredom, go to the casino. It's far less expensive. The public used to watch us from the visitor's gallery and we all looked engaged in a rush of something. But that is a misleading appearance. In actual fact, we are making money, one small profit at a time. Go ahead, call it boring if you like, Mr. Preacher. If you are afraid of boring, you are in trouble. The truth is that it is work, hard work. And the

---

[95] Frankly, I am ashamed that a preacher would take a free shot at our industry by calling it boring. He didn't even cite a scripture to back it up. I cite more scripture in a chapter on trading than he does in a whole sermon. Embarrassing. Do you suppose Edison was bored after trying a hundred different materials for the light bulb? What about two hundred? Three hundred? Small wonder Christianity gets a bad name.

profit is earned, not won by luck, clairvoyance, or wizardry. And when some preacher tells you that your calling in life is boring, leave, cheer up, read the bible for yourself, and start thinking of all the good things you can do with the offering you won't be placing in his plate. I have already mentioned my questionable relationship with members of the cloth. One clergyman terminated our friendship simply because he knew full well that I had something negative on my mind. People ignore negative things to their peril. But that is merely my opinion. Some people make it their strategy in life to avoid the negative and focus exclusively on the positive. In our business, this is fatal.

CHAPTER SIX

A CHRISTIAN WITH FOUR ACES?

It looked like a normal day. I made my way across the draw-bridge over the Chicago River with a thousand other people, walked by Sears Tower, and headed toward Jackson and LaSalle. I didn't notice any of it, least of all the people, the crowded elevator to the 4th floor, or any of the greetings that were exchanged. Yesterday had been a nightmare. War had broken out somewhere and they didn't have the decency to wait until the market was closed to do it. I'd been buried in the panic and I wasn't the only one. I swapped my jacket for my trading coat, didn't look up at the quote boards high overhead, just headed straight for my trade checker. On the way past the corn pit I overheard someone say to a visitor, "You may not see much action today. Everyone is pretty shell-shocked from yesterday." Yeah, that summed it up for me, and I said to my-self, "I'll keep my hands down today. Maybe just trade one lot at a time."

I once met a trader in the restroom during a turbulent period. We exchanged a few how-ya-doings and he said, "I'm leaving for Florida. I can't trade this volatility."

I said, "C'mon. Don't leave now. This is when we need you the most."

He said, "I can't make money with these swings."

I said, "Cut your trading size in half and double your profit objective."

"I can't make that adjustment," he said. "I'm outa here."

It is not my role to criticize a fellow trader. Everyone has to trade in a way that meets their personal style. And during times like that or after a huge loss like many of us suffered when that war broke out,[96] there is nothing to do but trade smaller.

However, when you face the kind of drawdown we've been looking at in the last two chapters, the trade-smaller advice sounds like a joke. These drawdowns are of a magnitude that tries one's very soul. Some of you will take my advice and head for another line of work. Mediocrity in any other profession will be far more productive, and fun, than failure in this one.

Nevertheless, avoidance of our business will not enable you to escape the trauma of the past two chapters. It will just come in some other form. Suppose a close friend whom you trust to oversee your nest egg does a Ponzi scheme and leaves you with nothing. It happens. If you are a trader, your drawdown will likely be financial. But non-financial drawdowns can be worse.

In the first chapter, there was a reference to a review of an earlier book, with an allusion to Mark Twain. The reviewer wrote that Ritchie had the calm confidence of a Christian with four aces. They meant it as a compliment (I trust). As for Twain, we might assume that he knew the American proverb that a .357 magnum beats 4 aces. Twain's meaning is slippery. Presumably a Christian has confidence in something unseen while the aces are what really get the job done.

Now the question for us traders is how in the world do we get the confidence we need to trade in the middle of drawdowns

---

[96] Everyone thinks we floor traders have an inside track on the info. As usual, the opposite is the case. We are always the last ones to find out what happened. We are too busy creating and reacting to the panic to watch the news.

as drastic as what we've seen? We have no aces and the capital flows out like water.

It's an emotional question for sure, indeed a spiritual question. It will happen to you sooner or later.

Christian theory is that a person is a child of the creator of the universe and the creator has the best interest of his children at heart. These children, so called, are the laborers in his metaphorical vineyard who will reap an eternal reward upon meeting him when all this is over. Can you buy all that? It surely will not be an easy sell if it is preached by one who thinks that you are a merchant of greed. And it won't matter if you are a member of some other faith, or if you have no faith at all. You will still be put to the test. What's more, you will be blindsided by the testing agent—an innocuous, impersonal market that has a stranglehold on your valuables. Right?

If you are not in sync with me, you have not pictured yourself in the trauma of the last two chapters. You went to the mountaintop. You turned $100K into $250K, then back to $20K. The "trade-smaller" advice has done *nothing* for you. All you feel is a kinship with Job. There is not an ounce of calm confidence, no aces in sight, and the .357? Who the —- brought that up?[97]

Some of you are thinking this should be moved to the FYX. Not so. The fact that you may disagree with the conclusion does not negate the need to have a life foundation that can keep you going. Ignoring this chapter because the topic has never applied to you is like the guy who ignored his life insurance because the ROI was not meeting his minimum requirements. Okay, if that's too silly, there are more—remember the

---

[97] The .357 is a joke (the aces as well), by the way. But at a time like this, a gun is counterproductive. I had a friend who, in a moment of despair, called his friend and asked him to come over to his house and remove all his guns. When you are trying to sort things out at a difficult time in life, a handy gun will cloud, not clarify, your thinking. Although it can bring a quick and easy end to your problem, it is inconsiderate for the family in the extreme. Stop reading right now if you get woozy. Some guns do not put a hole in your head; they remove about half of it. I saw one once. Everything above the nose was gone. Whoever discovers you in this condition will never be the same again.

farmer who lost money on the hedge side of his business five years in a row? He quit hedging.

Better yet, who can forget that farmer who stopped farming because he was consistently making all his profit on his hedge?

Or what about the reverse? What about those savvy investors, with all due diligence, who upped their holdings with Bernie Madoff because the ROI was so smooth and consistent over time.[98]

For you traders still with me, it is not my goal to motivate you to become theologians for a chapter. No—my goal is to make you a better trader. And if you are a trader who has never needed this chapter, great. That means your drawdown will not come in the form of a margin call. This could be even uglier. Please trust me, you will need this chapter sometime between now and the payoff on your life insurance.

Let me review, because I know that you will not be convinced that in the middle of a book about trading we need a chapter giving out arguments for Christianity. In the last chapter, we traded everything right and we failed because we stopped in the wrong place. But if we had continued, we would have made a billion dollars. The solution to our woulda-coulda-shoulda problem was simply a matter of certitude. Yes, we needed to control our spending and I made that point. But I also made the point that no human being could have traded through that volatility without super-human confidence.

It will not matter how you were raised, you still must travel down a road that will give you certitude about who you are, what you believe, and where you are headed. Remember C.W. Moss, Bonnie and Clyde's partner in crime? Bonnie asked about his family upbringing. He said, "Disciples of Christ." Presumably he skipped the journey about which I speak, took the easy path, and became a murderer.

---

[98] You can thank me now. If I told all these stories, the fluff in this book would expand the page count to 1000.
THE POINT: Short-term results are not the be-all, end-all of evaluations.
THE COROLLARY: The shorter the term, the less reliable the results.

If you want to be a trader, you need to finish this trip. If you intend to survive the downs of the last chapter, you must find certitude in your calling.

Imagine for a moment my speculating hero, Joseph, at the beginning of harvest number seven. He has gone through a pile of Pharaoh's money with six years of price supports for farmers. He's built another new silo every year for the past five years. And the local stand-up comedy about Hebrews, misers, and hoarding of grain has gotten to him. The price continues to fall. Sometime in the middle of that seventh harvest he goes back to Pharaoh and says, "Maybe we should review that dream one more time."

I can't speak for Joseph, but I know me pretty well. And from that, I can extrapolate a few things about you. If you don't have the spiritual foundations of your life pretty well set, the self-doubt alone will end your trading, possibly not right away, but sometime.

First: Let us give thanks that we are in America. In America everyone is whatever he wants to be—Christian, Jew, Moslem, Buddhist, Atheist, Hindu, Satanist, Mormon, Scientologist, Tao-ist, New Age, Deist, Naturalist, Nihilist, Existentialist, Pantheist, Sikh, Animist, Shintoist or Nothing.[99] That's the list. There's more, but you should be in there. That is what it means to be an American; you are free to be and think whatever you like.

Second: We are discussing trading, emotional disasters, and worse. We are struggling with the critical issue that no other investing book will tell you about, i.e., the crisis that every trader will face sooner or later. And this means that wherever you fall on that list I gave you in the last paragraph, it will get reviewed at that time.

Therefore: My goal in this chapter is to give you an example of how I have answered the question. Your disagreements are

---

[99] We have capitalized *Nothing* because in America you can make up your own nothingness and register it with the IRS as a church. (I am going to submit this to Wikipedia as an illustration to help them describe the vernacular use of "nuts.")

welcome. That's what we do in America. But I need you to see that such a foundation is possible. So when the dung hits the fan (as we say), you will not be caught without a cogent leg to stand on. So in whatever group you fall, you must do something to solidify your foundation in that mindset.

We all know that it is not politically correct to be argumentative about matters of faith. I'm sorry. If you cannot be argumentative, at least with yourself, you will never achieve any certitude about anything. Here is how I have done it.

Because there are entire sections of libraries devoted to this topic, let me do what any trader would do—reduce the whole matter to its lowest common denominator.

For a Christian, like me, there are only two things about which I need to be certain:

ONE: There is a God
TWO: There was an incarnation.

You may note that Christian people consider these to be articles of faith. That's fair enough, but it is misleading, and no help to a trader. The phrase, "articles of faith," is not consistent with the call for proof. Are we going to accept these two foundations of Christianity based on faith, or based on evidence?

You must know by now that I don't accept much on faith. I need evidence. So to label these two items, "articles of faith," is a misunderstanding of the word. This may turn out to be a minority opinion.

One prof referred to this as faith in faith. He may have even written a book by that title. The new rage of the past half century has been presuppositionalism. (Academics love to expand the dictionary.) It means that you presuppose all of the scripture, sort of like an axiom in geometry. Then if it proves to be useful and never breaks down, it must be true.

And there's more. Some religious people suppose that the greater one's faith, the greater one's ability to believe the unreasonable. It seems that once we step into the realm of religious worldviews, almost anything goes. I've heard all of the following lines:

There is no God and I'm prejudiced against him.

There is no God and I hate him.

There is no God and Jesus Christ is his son.

There is no God and Mary is his mother. The great philosopher, George Santayana said that one.

Now please do not let me or anyone else belittle your faith or any of the good feelings it may produce. But where we are going, your warm feelings will never get you through. I doubt this sort of faith is valid for anything, but that's beside the point right now.

For me, I have only one word for all this: Nonsense. Josling's critique of *God in the Pits*[100] makes far more sense to me than any of these approaches to faith. This is where religion gets its slipperier-than-oil reputation. People think they gain some advantage with some deity somewhere by believing the unbelievable. I agree with my atheist professor who said that if you want to believe something like the resurrection, you better be willing to accept the burden of proof. It seems obvious that a retreat to faith is a mistake. That scholar who coined the phrase, faith in faith, only piled the foolishness higher. This kind of thinking may work on Friday if you're Moslem, Saturday if you're Jewish, and Sunday if you're Christian. But on Monday when the margin call comes in, you are in deep trouble.

For purposes of brevity, let me summarize the most compelling arguments for these two claims. Then I will refer the reader to two contemporaries of mine who have studied, written, and debated these topics with far greater lucidity than have I.

---

[100] See his one-star review on Amazon. I had intended to respond to it in this book, but space will not allow. I have responded to it in some detail on Amazon. Josling is wrong, but he's thinking. That's a compliment and a requirement for trading.

First: There is a God

This is the easy one. Nevertheless, one must admit that it is slippery. It is like trying to prove the existence of water to a fish. It is so obvious that it is easily missed.[101] The evidence for the theistic claim exists in every atom, every blade of grass, every star in the universe. The stereotype that science and God are at odds is surely a mistake of the highest order.

Bertrand Russell made a fundamental point to his generation. He admitted the need for something that was eternal and said it is just as easy to believe that the universe is eternal. Thus we do not need an eternal being such as God.

Then along came science and demonstrated that the universe is not eternal. It had a beginning just as the nonscientific people of faith had thought.

Darwin supposed that life came about spontaneously. Science showed otherwise.

Scientists speculated about the recapitulation of the human fetus. Science showed otherwise.

The leading atheist of the past century, Anthony Flew, required reading by all of us philosophy students, gave up his atheism at the age of eighty. He attributed his change to the advance of science in the area of DNA. He said that the unbelievable complexity that science had discovered forced him to become a believer.

No scientist who ever lived has ever discovered anything about the universe and said to herself, "The universe would have been better if this formula were slightly different." Allan Sandage made the observation that every atom in the brain you are using right now was once inside a star. Indeed, we now know that every atom inside every star was once nothing. Many will say that the gaps in our knowledge that used to be explained by God are closing. In fact, as we close the gaps in our knowledge, what we really learn is that there is much more wisdom in the universe than we once knew. Josling is right that

---

[101] It is a guess on my part that providence has made theism easy to overlook. Pascal is credited with this observation.

natural selection does explain improvements made over time by all the species. But it can never explain the perfection of the planetary motion, gravity, or a host of other phenomena, indeed, any other phenomenon. It cannot explain the origin of the first cell, mistakenly thought to be simple.

And when I ask a scientific naturalist how long it will take my family tree to develop an eye in the back of our heads, they don't take me seriously. We all agree that we are more advanced than the mosquitoes that we kill. Yet primitive as they are, they still have as many eyes as I do. What could possibly explain this? I also ask them about a watch for my wrist. I need a sweep second hand, a light, an alarm, and a stopwatch. These items make me much more efficient. How long will it take my descendants to grow these on their wrists?

Then here is my question for you: Why does the naturalist think that I'm not serious when I ask these questions? The watch I need is not nearly as complex as the wrist I have already developed by natural selection. If natural selection did the wrist for me, it should be no problem to do the watch.

The difficulty is to think, or believe, that there could exist a being that is capable of creating all that we see. Naturally, it is no small challenge to the human mind to imagine this.

On the other hand, how difficult is it to imagine that such wonder happened all by itself? It is far beyond comprehension. Faith? How could anyone need faith to believe that there must be an efficient cause of all this. The concepts here reviewed have nothing to do with faith. This is a discussion of common sense. The alternative to theism is simply devoid of an explanation.[102]

---

[102] I left my house for a moment of solitude to finish the edit on this chapter, drove to a nearby forest preserve, and sat at a picnic table in a small shelter. On a stroll by my shelter were a pair of sandhill cranes. I had never seen one up close. It is safe to assume that all readers will agree with me on one point—this was a scene of beauty. Alan Sandage spent his life looking at the stars. You can see his pics on the internet. He has not found an ugly one yet. I'm not sure about this, but I doubt that you would know the meaning of the word ugly if there were no God. (I returned here to add that I just heard the most amazing sound, six or seven whooshes in rhythm—wings fanning air, gaining lift. It was those huge cranes struggling to gain altitude as they took off, just clearing the

But allow me to pose a question even more basic than the evolution of life, a question that only the theist can answer: How did natural selection ever get started? We know there was a time when it wasn't. Darwin didn't invent it; he only discovered it. Then who thought it up and set it in motion? The skeptic can only hope that it needs no explanation; this is just the way things are, they will say. This is my point. Things just "happen" to be working very well, awfully close to perfect. This is also what the author of Genesis wrote.

If you are in sharp disagreement with me, you must give this some time to settle in. I'd been thinking about it for years when the light finally dawned. It can only be described as an epiphany, a moment when one sees the truth for one's self. I'd heard someone say that every blade of grass proves the existence of God. It never sunk in. Here's what happened to me:

It was a hot day in Colorado and I was cooling myself with a drink and staring at the ice in my glass. My mind wandered (nothing new there). I asked myself, "Why is that ice floating?" Everyone knows that the water in the bottom of the lake is colder than the water at the top; cold stuff is always lower, it doesn't matter what it is. The simple law of hot things expanding is universal. Then why does freezing water break pipes? I understand why boiling water breaks pipes. Everyone knows that. But freezing water? Someone schooled me; nothing very complex here. The rules of expansion and contractions get reversed in H_2O at 39 degrees. Really? I thought. How convenient is that? Every body of water in the world should be freezing from bottom up, destroying life as we know it.

No wonder we need an infinite number of universes to explain how this one got so lucky. Remember the infinite monkeys and the infinite typewriters? It also explains why holy writ accuses the unbeliever of not thinking. Because I was

---

top of my shelter.) Incidentally, Sandage, the great astronomer, became a Christian at the age of sixty. I can assure you it had nothing to do with faith in faith. "Day after day they [the heavens] pour forth speech. Night after night they display knowledge." (Psalm 19:2) His conversion resulted from the truth he learned watching "creation."

thinking about this rule, which could just as easily be described as a miracle, and I could imagine no reason for this rule to exist, I could only conclude that someone very bright had caused it to be this way.[103]

I began to reflect on every rule of science that I'd ever heard. Each one was just as brilliant as this one. There is little doubt that it is tricky to imagine a being smart enough and powerful enough to do all that theism needs him to do. But the alternatives are not available.

Before I proceed to the second and much more difficult point, let me remind you again that we are discussing the matter of Ritchie's confidence in his foundation, the four aces. You must do the same, even if your worldview is solipsism.[104] Even if you are Nothing, you will need good evidence to support yourself in the middle of those bad times.

Second: There was an incarnation

Theism was the easy part; almost everyone in that widely diverse list of worldviews agrees with theism. The space was given to it in order to show that theism is not a matter of faith, but a matter of fact.

Now the plot thickens. While the vast majority of that long list agrees with theism, an even larger majority deny the incarnation. Remember please–I am not taking a detour into theology. I'm giving you my source of certitude that enables one to endure one of those drawdowns of the last chapters. Thus my criticism of faith; but more on that in the FYX.

You know by now that I grew up with Moslems. I was conversing one day with a Moslem friend and happened by chance to mention that his God, Allah, surely had the power to

---

[103] Science can only inform us that H_2O works this way. But science cannot explain how it happens. And when they do explain how it happens, this will only show the wisdom of God. It will not show him to be unnecessary.

[104] Sorry–I could not resist. The word came up in a jeopardy game, so I had to throw it in. This is the view that I am the only one here. And I am imagining all of you. This is classic ivory tower work. And we should be giving thanks that all of us are too busy being productive to learn words like this one.

spend time in his world and enter it through the birth canal.[105] His body literally shuddered in reaction to my use of the words, "Allah, through the birth canal." One has to admit, this is an awesome thought.

I mentioned my atheist prof at Portland State University who said, "If you want to make a claim like a resurrection, you are going to have to accept the burden of proof." We have and will continue to make the point of the mistake of atheism. But not everything an atheist says is wrong; and not everything a Christian says is correct. It is Christians who are most susceptible to missing this important point, no compliment to us. In this case, the atheist is spot on.

The homework that is called for at this point gives me a slight advantage over what you will call *normal* people. You see, I'm a murder mystery junkie. And Christianity presents us with the greatest murder mystery case in the history of mystery cases. The body was missing.

Allow me a quick summary of the evidence that has been sufficient to convince so many over the centuries. Then I will turn you over to those other authorities.

The body was missing. If his enemies could have produced it, they would have paraded it through the streets. He had no shortage of enemies—true then, and true today. So if he did not come back from the dead, we must assume that his friends hid the body and concocted the story of all stories with which to make themselves famous. This is a good theory, originated on Easter morning and still playing well. My prof summarized it when he said, "Who cares what they did with it. They could have chopped it in a thousand pieces and thrown it into Galilee for all we know."

The atheist is right, again, but *only* if they had made themselves famous and lived the high life of a celebrity TV evange-

---

[105] I wrote the word "friend" out of deference to him. A Moslem from Asia would call me, or you, a "friend" when we Westerners would still be using the word, "acquaintance." By the time we Westerners would say "friend," he would be saying "brother." This is a compliment to both parties, but the lion's share of it goes to the Moslem.

list. In that case, the theory has possibilities. We know that the disciples had visions of grandeur for themselves.[106] Maybe that is what they hoped for. The problem is that their enemies had other plans for them. There was no grandeur. Most of them wound up on crosses during which time not one of them spilled the truth about where they hid the body. If they had given up that truth, they could have gone from the torture of a crucifixion to the grandeur they sought, and in a few short minutes. But no. Tradition says that it took three days for Andrew to die—a little like water boarding on steroids. When one considers the ease with which a good interrogator can break down a conspiracy with a small amount of pressure, it is impossible to believe that these eleven fellows could have pulled off this hoax.

One needs a bit of an imagination to follow the hoax logic. One has to image a group of fishermen on the shore of Galilee laying out quite a plan. One of them says, "Why don't we add the doctrine of the atonement to all these other lies?" Peter, James, and John look at the guy, whoever he is, with astonishment. And the guy adds, "We'll say he died for the sins of the world. If they are dumb enough to believe a resurrection, why not do a big one? The Goyim will love it. Which one of us will write this up?" To discount the resurrection, that is what had to happen. Given the deaths they all died, that scenario is unimaginable.

The details to which I have referred are what caused academy award winning filmmaker, William Peter Blatty to say, "If it weren't true, then Jesus Christ is a liar. And all his apostles were liars. And I don't think that's likely." You may assume from that statement that he is a believer. But at the very least, he has not appealed to faith as his reason for belief. He has given a reasoned conclusion from the evidence.

But if you are inclined to discount a believer, let me appeal to the late Rabbi Pinchas Lapide, the Orthodox Jew who wrote *The Resurrection of Jesus*. Lapide never converted to Christianity. Nevertheless, the details surrounding that first century event

---

[106] Matt 20:21; Mk 10:37

were so compelling that he concluded that Jesus must have returned from the grave.

TWO AUTHORITIES FOR YOUR REVIEW

It was mentioned earlier that you will be directed to two authors for further review.

William Lane Craig

While struggling my way through these problems studying philosophy of religion, there was a guy who sat next to me in class. I would never expect Bill to remember me; he was too focused on the cosmological argument. We both went on after grad school. I became a lowly clerk at the CBT and he went to all those European institutions where one must philosophize in some other language. Then you earn letters after your name that require foreign accents to pronounce with propriety. You notice that I'm trusting he hasn't lost his sense of humor in all those libraries. Today, William Lane Craig has written enough to answer any additional questions you will surely have after this brief summary. And I would be remiss not to mention the mentor of both Bill and myself. The name Normal L. Geisler will keep popping up on your Google searches. Anything you read by him will prove helpful for sure. The only problem is that anyone reading my material will be intimidated by an author who wrote eighty books. He's still alive so that number will be obsolete by the time you read this.

Lee Strobel

The second person you need to know is another contemporary, one whom I have *not* met. But he's a product of my town and a former investigative reporter for the Chicago Tribune. Lee Strobel was challenged to do an honest investigation of the issues of this chapter. His writings will fill in the many blanks that my brevity must omit.

These two thinkers are my contemporaries. I have suggested that the notion that my faith is provable is a minority opinion. Nevertheless, the great writers of history, from Anselm to C.S. Lewis support my opinion. These two authors follow in that tradition.

Now that the name C.S. Lewis has come up, it must be mentioned that he found the evidence so compelling that he wrote that he was dragged kicking and screaming into the kingdom. Fine. He was a British gentleman. You know—the type who drink their tea with the pinky finger in the proper position. Lewis wrote figuratively. He probably never kicked or screamed in his entire life. We Americans are different, plus we don't build our walls out of stone like in Britain. The skeptic, Lee Strobel, actually did kick a hole in his wall while trying to avoid being dragged into the kingdom.

I am a person of very small faith. But when I arrive at that drawdown, I have not consumed even an ounce of my tiny faith in order to accept my worldview. The foundation of my personhood is based on objectively observable facts. This is critical because now I have all my faith, small as it is, available to trust that God is going to get me through this drawdown.

Of course, it will help to have a friend to remind you of these things at just the right time. My friend, Larry Burkett, did precisely that for me on one occasion when I had a position on that was strangling me and I had no idea where to get out. He gave me assurance of who I was, what I was about, and that I could have confidence in the future. I began liquidating the next morning and was back on track.

Someone said, "Seek and you will find." The fact is that many of you have not given enough time to seeking.

I've given you a summary of how I have arrived at what they referred to as calm confidence. Please know that I have never felt calm or confident in the middle of a drawdown. But it has still gotten me through a number of scrapes. Some of you will prefer to call it a crutch. I don't really care what you call it, the important thing is that it has kept me going when things have gotten rough.[107] That is what you will need as a trader. If you are in one of the alternative worldviews listed earlier, you will need to do as rigorous a homework to solidify your foundation as I have done. If you are a Christian, you still need to do it. If you think this is a matter of taste, upbringing, and personal preference, you are making a horrific mistake. If you are a Christian because you like Christmas or you are a member of an Eastern faith because you like turbans, you do not have a foundation that will support you through the draw-downs of our business.

---

[107] I hired a relative who worked for me for about six uneventful months. Then we had a wild day, and I do mean wild. We yelled, ran, carded, and counted at full speed from the opening to the closing bell. When it was over he said, "Mark, I have always thought you didn't work for a living."

FYX

Christian people have been so intimidated by the wisdom of science that they have retreated into believism. I made that word up. It is classically called fideism, meaning faithism. There are more academic ways to put it. Presuppositionalism might be the most academically respected order of the past half century.

If your faith is based on faith, you are not ready. If you think the bible is the word of God because it says it is, your footing is as feeble as everyone else on that list of world-views. All *their* writings claim to be the word of God. If you think the claim is sufficient to make it true, you have become the quintessential example for all future logic texts. "Begging the question" never had a better illustration. And this is no compliment.

I once met a leading evangelical pastor in my town, Chicago, who objected to my use of the cosmological argument for the existence of God. He said, "Then you have the problem of the infinite series of causes."[108] I was too shy to suggest that I did not have that problem.

Let us consider what holy writ has to say on the topic. "Come now, let us reason together,"[109] appears to be a call to rational thought. Why would Isaiah not just call for faith? When Nathanael told Andrew that nothing good comes from Nazareth, Andrew should have rebuked him for his lack of faith. But no. He said, "Come and see."[110] And why would Luke mention that Jesus had given "many convincing proofs that he was alive?"[111] Paul tops it all off with his claim that the

---

[108] Please do not think that I know or socialize with these celebrity men of God. I cross paths with them rarely, and get these priceless quotes. I'll admit to one close relationship with an evangelical celeb, Normal L. Geisler, with whom I've had a close friendship beginning four and half decades ago when he became my mentor. I also had a friendship with the late Larry Burkett. All other Christian celebs are unknown by me.

[109] Isaiah 1:18

[110] John 1:46 Natan'el answered him, "Natzeret? Can anything good come from there?" "Come and see," Philip said to him.

[111] Acts 1:3 After his death he showed himself to them and gave many convincing proofs that he was alive

divine being had given proof to all people by a resurrection from the dead?[112]

Certainly the scriptures speak highly of faith, but not of blind faith, not of faith that comes from nothing. Many Christians have supposed that it is an act of righteousness to accept the bible as the infallible word of God. They make this as a starting point for knowledge.

Christians will recall "the great debate" between Bill Nye, the science guy, and Ken Ham the "young-earth" creationist.[113] Bill Nye won that debate when Ken Ham asserted, "We have different starting points. I begin with the bible as the word of God." I agree with many of Ham's positions—theism, intelligent design, and the now-scientifically-proven moment of creation. But his starting point for truth is a horrific mistake.

The claim that the bible is the word of God is a conclusion from all the facts of history that we have available to us. How could Nye have a meaningful dialogue with a person who assumes as a starting point the conclusion that he is trying to prove? In case this is not obvious: If you say that your starting point is that the bible is the word of God, you have assumed what you've set out to prove. Then when you give even one reason why the bible is the word of God, you no longer have an assumption.

If you have read down to here, you must be a Christian. You have taken up your cross and followed Christ, whatever the cost, found meaning and purpose to your existence, and secured your eternal destiny. You've done all this on an assumption? I'll pray for you.

After all that Thomas had seen, he still refused to believe. Yet Jesus made a special appearance just for him. Does this not show you that he is not expecting you to assume anything?

---

[112] Acts 17:31 And he has given public proof of it by resurrecting this man from the dead.

[113] It garnered great and immediate attention, great consternation by scientists, great attendance, and a few other greats. But the title, "great debate," could fade over time.

CHAPTER SEVEN

THE REST IS DETAILS

STOPS

A simple stop in the market will free your mind to work on important things. Let us suppose, for example, that you work out of your home. While this was extremely rare in my day, it is becoming more common. And this trend will surely continue as the computer and internet bring the market closer to us every year. So your kid runs into your office and interrupts your trading. You cannot give her any sort of attention because you are inexorably attached to your losing trade. I could make this side story much more interesting if it is your spouse in the middle of the day, kids all gone to school.

But it won't matter whether it is your kid, your spouse, or your next winning opportunity in the market, you will miss it because your mind is locked into your sick, losing trade. Whereas, if you'd like to be a winning trader, you won't be worrying about your positions in the market; **every position will have a stop to cover it**. Do you hear the volume in my voice? Your kid, spouse, or market-analysis gets all the attention necessary, because you are not focused on your positions. You are already covered. If you are really disciplined and organized, you might even have your profit objectives in the market too, each stop and objective on an OCO basis.

The stop is the best way you can verify with any certitude your maximum loss, and it will also help keep your average loss under control. You will learn this soon enough, so we might as well get to it now:

Anyone can take a profit; it requires a pro to take a loss.

And the corollary:

It is very difficult to go broke if your losses are well controlled.

Corollary #2:

Avoiding going broke will keep you in business.

DON'T TRADE WITH YOUR GUT

You may take this entire point as personal, idiosyncratic, or fickle. Suit yourself. But it is important to my personality type. This business will elicit a vast range of emotions. If you want to be a writer and try to reproduce those emotions in your readers, fine. But don't think for a moment that your feelings about a trade are of any value as an indicator. This is a cerebral business, not an emotional one. If you get an overwhelming feeling that the trade you are about to make has a foreboding over it, a feeling that things aren't going to go right, a misgiving, don't let that feeling affect your judgment. Some of the worst trades I've ever made looked like the best. I can still recall the great promise I felt as I executed some of those trades. But many turned out to be losses, even disastrous losses. And on other trades, I've often had some of the worst sense of foreboding.

On one unusually large trade, I could almost hear Mozart's rich minor chords from his Requiem (the hazard of musicianship). They would ring in my ears. What more could a trader, especially a Christian who talks to God, ever expect to receive as a sign to keep him out of trouble? Do you expect an angel to show up and warn you? Some of the trades responsible for this awful feeling in the gut turned out to be the best trades

I've ever made. Focus on the stats; focus on the probabilities; focus on a quality entry point. Don't go swinging around the market with your feelings.

SAMPLE TRADING IDEA
(entry and exit points)

You are forbidden to tell anyone about this. It should be hidden in a footnote. If they find out about this, they will skip all the important stuff, come straight here, and lose their money.[114]

By now you know that I cannot and will not give you an entry point. So how about one or two? Every rule has its breaking or bending point.

Here's the plan:
1. Compute two days range. Suppose soybeans had a 30 cent range over the past two days.
2. Multiply the range by .67. We're making this easy, 20 cents.
3. Add and subtract that number from today's close. Suppose it closed at 10.00, so add and subtract 20 cents.
4. Buy or sell tomorrow at that price. Buy at 10.20, sell at 9.80.
5. At the close, do the same computation for the next day. If you are in the market (say long at 10.20), you need only compute the sell point. Stop and reverse at the sell point.

Bruce Babcock called this system the volatility envelope. He said that he had seen it sold for $3,000 and saw Larry Williams sell it for $12,000–well, only $2,000 down and the rest out of profits.[115] I'll recommend Babcock's book to you, Schwager's too.

---

[114] I know you are not willing for another side story. But this one has to be told. I gave a strong recommendation to Schwager's first book in my first book. I'll give one here too, coming up soon. So a close friend, reading my pre-publication manuscript, immediately dropped my book, went out a bought Jack's book, and quickly lost all his money. Not some, all. He was too ashamed to tell me about it until years later. That was 25 years ago and he has not traded since. My book was jammed with warnings against such mistakes. I immediately deleted the name of Jack's book from that edition of *God in the Pits*.

[115] *Dow Jones Irwin Guide to Trading Systems*, Babcock, pp. 139-141. I've already waxed eloquent, or raved, on the matter of the purchase of systems.

These will get you very well started on your entry and exit career. There may be more, but you won't need any more than these two. After you get yourself launched into trading, you'll come up with all your own ideas that will fit your personality.

Now let's take a closer look. Babcock tested the system and it did great over five years in the 80s but avoided the '87 crash. That's a little selective, but surely the '87 crash would have messed up anybody's results. So you can't blame him for not including that. However, and this is huge, you want to know what the crash would do to you. I ran this system on current markets and could not find a winner. However, it is possible that some of my parameters were slightly different from his.

Nevertheless, let's look at his results. He tested ten markets. We will consider the second best of the ten, T-Bonds. Over the five years, this system did as follows:

Total trades	193
Winning trades	90
Winning percentage	47
Total profit	17,375
Average win	1,569
Average loss	969
Max Drawdown	13,418
Average profit per trade	214

You can see that the winning ratio was almost exactly what we used, only 3 percent shy of 50. And then a win-loss ratio of 1,569/969 make this an outstanding system. You would get wealthy with a system like this and it is no wonder that Williams was able to sell a bunch at whatever price. Run these number through my formula and you'll see that you can invest 14 percent of your capital on the strategy. It's a total winner.

Before you run out to start trading it, let me suggest a few possible problems with this winner:

Did your mother (maybe grandmother, these days) give you that if-you-can't-say-anything-nice-shut-up line? So I can't talk too much about system selling. Anyway, you can have this one for free.

First – Babcock fails to show us his max loss. I won't criticize. That is his style. His focus in on the max drawdown which is not so important to me. Because on every loss, I reduce my trade size on the next trade. So his huge worst drawdown of 13K will be reduced in my scheme. In fact, I would not even know how to calculate my trading size with his numbers because without a max loss I cannot know my risk on my first trade.

Second – This is a minor complaint, but this system does not trade very often, less than once per week. But the money is still tied up because it is always in the market.

Third – This complaint will kill his system and any system like it. If you look closely, you can see that your turnaround stopping point might not get hit on any given day. And the next day it moves. It might not get hit on that day either. In fact, if you got a slow and well-organized trend against your position, it might never get out. Lordy have mercy! Any questions?

Fourth – There is a built-in over-optimization factor that you must notice. This is one of the better of the 10 systems Babcock ran. Why did we choose it? Because it was better than eight of the others. Fine. That is over-optimizing. You must look out for that.

After observing that third complaint, you must agree that our first foray into entries and exits will have to go back to the drawing board. This does not mean it is a bad idea. It means that the system is not going to come close to standing alone.

Now the punch line to the exercise: I use this system. I cannot recall where I got it, but most likely from Babcock back in the 80s. But I use it as a filter, maybe to help with market entry. I certainly don't use it to give me any stops. I like short stops that are volatility sensitive, just like this system *could* give you. Although these stops are not short. And a volatility stop can be huge in a wild market. I cannot stand a system that might surprise me with a sudden huge stop. So I will have a large protective dollar stop for wild markets and a small volatility stop that will get me out at a small loss during quiet times.

BOOK REVIEWS

Two books will get you started and may be all you will need. Then another two will have you swimming in the deep water with specific buy and sell ideas and philosophies that have undergone decades of execution in real markets.

Bruce Babcock, Jr's
The Dow Jones Irwin Guide to Trading Systems

Probably the best intro to system development that you will find, a much easier read that Schwager's. It will give you a great beginning into the development of entry and exit points. However, be warned, none of these books provide you with your cookie cutter trading ideas that will do all the thinking for you, as you just saw with my analysis of Babcock's or Williams' volatility envelope.

Jack Schwager's
A Complete Guide to the Futures Market

After meeting Jack and doing an interview for one of his many sequels, we had a friendly disagreement.[116] I said that his "Complete Guide" could not be topped no matter how many wizards he interviewed. He said that the wizard series would far surpass the "Complete Guide." If sales are what you are about, he was right. If understanding the market is your thing, I stand by my original opinion. But I admit that the book buyers think nothing of my opinion. One must wonder if he was running out of wizards. Every time you take a loss, you don't feel very wizard-like.

---

[116] When traders disagree, pay special attention. You seldom have to pick a side. We disagree in a way that we can both be right. Also the reverse is equally true. The best story on this is about two traders, one of whom I knew reasonably well. They stood in the middle of the bean pit and discussed their long position, each one assuring the other of a wide variety of reasons why this market was on the upswing. While they were talking Richard yelled, "Sold! Sold! Sold!" to three different traders and liquidated 500 beans in a few seconds. His friend said, "What are you doing? We just agreed this thing has to go higher!" Richard said, "I figure we can't both be right."

Mark Minervini's
Trade Like a Stock Market Wizard

I've traded plenty of stocks, but not in the Minervini method. Thus I cannot give a detailed analysis. However, I've watched a fellow trader utilize Minervini's methods with a lot of success. Endorsements are cheap and flow like water. But an endorsement that shows up on the equity statement can be relied on with confidence that is hard to come by in this industry.

Peter Brandt's
Diary of a Professional Commodity Trader: Lessons from 21 Weeks of Real Trading

A few years back I wrote that I love the one-star reviews of my work Amazon. They reveal miscommunications, mysterious emotions, or simply ignorance.[117] Of course we authors love the five-star jobbies. But the one-star writers can be especially revealing. To illustrate this point, allow me to simply quote from Amazon's one-star reviews of Brandt's book.

The first one-star reviewer wrote that Brandt's book was, "a bunch of lines drawn on charts, with a bunch of 'what if's' attached." If you don't like 'what if's,' you won't like trading.[118]

The next one-star reviewer said, "I am shocked to see that after so many claimed years of trading that this read as little more than an armchair rookie with 6 months backing him." The reviewer claimed to have reviewed over 200 books on this topic, an amazing achievement. I cannot tell you to stop reading. Here you are. But sooner or later you must trade. That is where the serious learning will begin.

Here's the problem: Writers write. Traders trade. I have never met anyone who did both very well. If drawing lines on graphs bores you, so what? Are you expecting Brandt to hone his writing skill in order to captivate and hold your attention?

---

[117] An anthropology professor once said about one of my books, *"Spirit of the Rainforest* is a bunch of crap."* When a PhD resorts to that style, an author can be confident that his work has forced the academic out of his comfort zone.

[118] BTW—life is a long series of "what-ifs." Try to adjust and deal with it.

We call this business "work," not "fun." Brandt has decades of success behind him. I know no other trader with that many decades of success who is making an honest attempt to share his strategy. You will get yourself a good start on your career if you can follow the advice of such a trader.

The third one-star reviewer wrote, "not too interesting. If your [sic] looking for a pep talk on how to trade in commodities, this book is not it." Are you observing a trend in these one-star reviews? It must be assumed that any reader looking for a pet talk round-filed this book a few chapters back. But in case I'm wrong about that—How can you tell a genuine professional trader from the smooth-talking phony trader?[119] There is a punch line coming, but no comedy. The smooth-talker gives you a pep talk.

No pro trader will *ever* give you a pep talk. We are petrified that you will lose your money, all of it. Why do you suppose the book you are reading has encouraged you repeatedly to find another line of work? This is a dangerous business, having produced numerous suicides. If "not too interesting," and "pep talks" are on your radar screen, drop this book now and don't look back.

And the fourth one-star review from Amazon writes that Brandt's book should be called, "Diary of a Professional Mediocrity Trader." Never overlook a compliment that masquerades as an insult. If your trading feels mediocre, you may have achieved the consistency which will serve you well. Boring days in the black—I've had many of them. I thank God for them. I wish the same for you. This is a boredom you can come to love.

I had never met or spoken to Brandt[120] before I started writing this book. But because my son had been following his trading style, I contacted Brandt and requested his critique of this manuscript. Since that time I've crossed paths with a

---

[119] With great sorrow I inform you that there are a lot of these people.

[120] Actually I did recall his name. He made news in our trading community back in the 80s when he sleep-walked off his balcony. As I've said before, life delivers drawdowns in a variety of styles.

number of traders who credit Brandt with substantially improving their trading. That's an endorsement you cannot top. You can connect with him at: PeterLBrandt.com

MOVIE REVIEWS

Boiler Room

This one is surprisingly accurate, but only for a small part of our industry, one which I crossed briefly. I lasted about four hours in it. Fortunately this side of the industry gets all the bad press, which it earns. Nothing in this book is preparing you for this side of the industry. Nothing. Indeed, it only now occurs to me that there are two very different uses of the word "sell." You have been reading about buying low and selling high. I have spent exactly half of my career selling. However, if you use the word "sell" as it is most often used, as it is used in this movie, I could never sell anything to anyone. The people in this movie do not trade. They sell. You must know the difference by now. Ninety-nine percent of the people in the financial world sell. The other one percent trade.

This movie is a good representation of the way everyone in the selling world gets compromised.

The Wolf of Wall Street

First, the apology—for even watching this movie. Comparing "The Wolf of Wall Street" to our industry is like comparing Herman Gosnell[121] to the industry of Hippocrates.

Second, the important theme of the movie. The story is about human nature and how easily it is compromised. As usual, it is what you don't see that I find important. In this movie, it was the people who gave it an R-rating. They were at least as compromised as any character in the movie. The film industry can make up all the X-rated characters they like; we are still committed to running an honorable industry. The 9-11 attack

---

[121] In case you missed it, Dr. Gosnell is the physician who now serves a term for his abortion practices that the jury concluded were more like infanticide.

brought us down to a pile of rubble. We opened for business seven days later. Our business is not well served by an industry that characterized us as they did in this movie.

The movie had a memorable line, "the chickens had come home to roost, whatever the f--- that means." This wisdom came from the lead character, the good guy. The chickens coming home is the setup. The real wisdom is found in the revelation that he doesn't know what it means. In the business of "vengeance is mine," he hasn't seen nothin' yet.

The selling point is the same as "Boiler Room." Any of my readers knows this by now. There are traders and there are salespeople. Traders buy low and sell high. Salespeople only make money when they sell something for more than they paid for it, almost always more than what it is worth. That is the only way they can make money. I have known a host of professional traders throughout my career. I have never known one of them to ever "sell" anything to anybody. The trader's job, your job, is to initiate every trade away from (perceived) value and liquidate it at value. You will never initiate a trade at (perceived) value. Wouldn't that be a waste of time and effort?

I once asked the trainer of these sales people what I should do if the client wanted to liquidate the "great deal" I sold him. He told me to "eff" off. Maybe he found work as a consultant for this movie. I heard they set the F-word record, 550 times or more, depending on the speed and talent of your F-word clicker.

Trading Places

This is a good one. Duke and Duke portray the salespeople of the industry. Actual trading is about as treacherous as the movie portrays. The bathroom scene in anticipation of the opening bell was pretty realistic. The cheating on the crop report was also okay. There was once a guy who worked on the crop reporting staff. Their report never came out until after the market was closed. At about noon he would go to the window and adjust the shade; up meant small acreage, bull market tomorrow; down meant big acreage, selloff tomorrow; and middle of the window meant that the acreage would be just as expected. This movie capitalized on that issue and made for a great plot. I never got any such advance information, but have surely fantasized about how nice it would be.

The subplot: Are traders born or are they made? You want the answer to that one. You need the answer to that one. You have been analyzing this question about yourself since you picked up this book. And the answer is: Both. If I had worked as hard at playing baseball as the Hall of Fame great, Hank Aaron, I would have extended my playing career a year or two after college, but not to the Hall. If Aaron had been "blessed" with my athletic abilities, you would never have heard his name. But he still had to do the work to accomplish all he did. My hope is that this book will help you make the call about yourself and give you motivation and direction to get the job done.

TRADER'S CONTRASTING VIEWS

I mentioned that trader disagreement is an opportunity you ought not miss. Different personalities take risk differently. Below you will find Mark Minervini's trading rules. Minervini is a highly respected market wizard. I'm reading his rules off his coffee mug, which I drink from as I write this. I'll rate them on a 1 to 10 scale, 10 being the most effective.

"Approach every trade from risk first"

TEN. If you haven't figured this one out by now, you must have started reading on this page. It goes without saying that there was some profit motive to look at the trade in the beginning. But after that, your first focus must be on risk. Do not do business with a person who asks, "What could go wrong?" as if your venture is a sure deal.

"Don't risk more than you expect to gain."

ONE. See what I told you; trading is personality driven. This rule is a matter of Minervini's personal taste.[122] The vast majority

---

[122] I got a note from Minervini claiming that we are in far more agreement on this rule and the next two than I have noted with the "one, three, and five." I

of trades I've made in my career violated this rule. Don't deny your personality. Don't try to trade like Mark Ritchie *or* Mark Minervini. You must trade in a way that fits your personality. If you risk 10 ticks to make 5 ticks, you are trading my style. If you risk 5 tics to make 10 tics, you are trading Minervini's style. If you risk 5 tick to make 100 to 500 ticks, you are trading Richard Dennis' style. All these styles are viable. I don't care what style you trade. I just want you to be profitable. Get a style you are comfortable with. You can see that with my style, your winning percent will have to be much higher than with the Minervini or Dennis style. They can get by with a much lower winning percentage. Who cares about that? What we want is for you to develop a style that is comfortable for you and consistently profitable over the long term.

"Cut your losses quickly when they're small."

THREE. I'm rating this one low because my style would call for you to have a stop in the market as soon as your entry point is filled. Thus there should be no need for you to be thinking about cutting your loss quickly. The market will make this decision for you.

"Move your stop to break-even as soon as possible."

FIVE. You can see that I'm not ranking this one great because again, it is a matter of style. There is nothing wrong with this rule. If you hate losses, this one is for you; go ahead and give it your own rating of ten. But you will need to take many small losses and many scratch trades if you want to ever ride a trend. NOTHING WRONG WITH THAT STYLE.

---

believe the details in his book will support his position. You can't get too specific on a coffee mug. See my comment on his book coming up. Get his book and judge for yourself. *Trade Like a Stock Market Wizard: How to Achieve Super Performance in Stocks in Any Market.* His trading style has significantly influenced Mark II's trading; that is the ultimate endorsement. See Chapter Eight. Also, refrain from trying to learn trading by reading a coffee mug.

"Only increase trading size after you log a profit."

TEN. If you did not say, "Duh," you have skipped to this chapter. Why this is not self-evident remains a mystery, and provides the demand for this book. When else would one increase trading size? If you can think of another time, get another book and find another career. (Review chapter four if you need mathematical proof of Minervini's point.)

"Always have a contingency plan for everything."

TEN. Who can argue with this? If you have a stop-loss order in the market, it will save you having to be a genius and consume your valuable time in the development of contingency plans.

"Never average down—losers average losers."

TEN (for your first two years of trading) FIVE (after that) I've done this a lot. There is nothing wrong with doing it. EG, say I buy at 15 with a stop at 10. Then I buy again at 12 and put my stop at 7. If I consider the second buy a chance to get a better buying average, I have violated Minervini's rule and am setting up for a huge disaster. But if I'm operating two very different trading strategies, each with its own stop, each with its own history, there may be a place for this. However, one must realize that twice the risk is being taken when this happens. I would not do this until you have a few years' experience and a few hundreds trades under your belt.

"Avoid style drift—be a specialist in your approach."

TEN. Stay focused on the kinds of trades with which you are comfortable. Don't be changing your style every week. I met a guy who re-optimized his systems each weekend. You can elevate inconsistency to an art form and it will still be inconsistent. And do not under any circumstance pay attention to those guys who have some hot strategy to beat the market. They talk; you trade.

"Nail down profits—the goal is to make money."

TEN. Yes, take the money and run. However, please understand that this is not the traditional way to succeed in this business. The saying goes, "You can never go broke taking a profit." But you can never stay on a trend with this strategy either. You may *trade* with the trend, but you will never *ride* the trend with this strategy. If you are an investor, get on the trend and don't take your profits. But if you want to be a trader, this is the rule for you. You statisticians will want to run some numbers on this point. The faster you get out of the market and get on to another trade, the faster you compound your profits. Minervini's mantra would be, "Never underestimate the power of small profits multiplied over time." Indeed.

"Know the truth—conduct post analysis regularly."

I recuse myself from scoring this one because it hits my area of incompetence. But it looks like an invaluable idea if you can pull it off. As a floor trader, any attempt to do this was so fraught with hindsight, regret, 20-20 second guessing, and more, that it just gave rise to frustration and the constant muttering of "woulda-coulda-shoulda," a phrase we would like to grow out of. But trading from the screen will surely lend itself far more to this kind of analysis. My son, a student of Minervini's, has elevated this rule to an art form. See the next chapter.

MONEY IS THE ROOT OF ALL EVIL

I could not close without throwing this one in. You must understand that truth has a way of getting bent, damaged, and distorted at every turn. No sane person ever said this. There are a host of crimes that have nothing to do with money. The line originated when the Apostle Paul wrote his protégé a warning to the rich. He said, "The love of money is a root of all kinds of evil." Money is not the problem. Misplaced love is the problem, the result of which is a wide variety of bad things.

LIAR LIAR, PANTS ARE BURNING[123]

I want my friend and trusted colleague to write a book that would describe in detail the path he followed. He was at one time a God-fearing righteous wannabe who followed God with all his heart. A few years later he was discovered to be a totally lying thief. You and I could learn a lot about ourselves if we could see the play-by-play on how that happened. I'll ask you: Would you buy that book? I would. Because the phrase, "There but for the grace of God go I," applies to all of us except the extremely proud. I'll admit that I would very much like to observe the early signs of evolution into a liar.

It is my contention that most liars do not know that they are doing it. This should make it easier for them to confess. Just say, "I didn't actually realize that I became a liar. It happened while I wasn't looking." Go ahead—LOL. But there is a tiny bit of truth in this lame excuse. It could be happening to all of us.

Indeed, the problem has risen to the level of an epidemic at this time. In one state they passed a law against lying about one's military record. The court struck it down. They thought it was an infringement on the right to free speech.

The people I have worked with and traded with all my career are not liars. But they are rare. I mentioned in the first chapter my real estate broker, the late John Keepper. He is not a liar. And I put a footnote there naming all the brokers I have traded with who are not liars. The list expanded until it was so long that I had to leave it out. I am blessed. I have money in my possession today, decades later, that proves they are not liars.

Nevertheless, that long list may be too short. You have read here many stories of those who have been less than honest. Let's avoid reviewing old wounds and take another approach.

A broker once asked me, "What's wrong with telling all the positive points and avoiding the negative?" If your reaction to that question is not "Duh," you may have moved down that delusive path toward lying, quite unwittingly of course.

---

[123] The most beautiful girl I ever dated used this line on me once and I have been enjoying it ever since. Let's see if you share my sense of humor.

It is my opinion that most liars have fallen into the habit without noticing. This is not moralizing. If you are in this habit, it will have a deleterious effect on your trading, as a result of the lies you will tell yourself.

Here's what I need you to do: Take thirty days. After each conversation you have with another person, especially if you are convincing them of something, write a very short summary of what you said. Of course this applies if you are selling something, say a used car. But it applies to any conversation. In almost every conversation, you are persuading the other party of something, even if it is as innocuous as tomorrow's weather.

Then, a few hours later, you will review your summary and ask yourself this question: If I were on the other side of this conversation, would I be happy with the way that opinion was represented to me? This is nothing more than the golden rule applied to conversational discourse.

Some years back I met a broker and we did quite a bit of business together. He was a Christian who was serious about this faith and sought my help to do business as honorably as possible, like the accountability I mentioned earlier. Yet he could tell that I was not completely comfortable with his business style. His answers to my questions were not as straight and simple as what I was accustomed to. So I gave him the challenge that I just described. I told him to apply the golden rule to his summary of each conversation. About a month passed and he called me back. I had forgotten the challenge. He said, "Mark, I'm the biggest liar I have ever met. How have I missed it?" That is when it dawned on me how easy it is to become a liar without noticing.

Commerce in America requires truthfulness. I don't care what the Supreme Court says about free speech, if we are not truthful with each other, the cost of doing business will go up—a lot. Most readers will not worry about this, assuming that it is only wealthy business people who will be hurt. What a misunderstanding that is. Every financial inefficiency hurts everyone and the less one makes, the greater the impact.

FYNon-believers

This is a sad tone on which to close a chapter. So let us dispense with the FYX and issue a challenge to you non-believers. I need to challenge you to be far more aggressive in confronting us Christians about our hypocrisy. Hear me out; this is important.

Back in the early days, a group of us traders, Christians all, had a fine friend, Michael Moss, with whom we hung out. We called him the Mystery Moss because he gathered information around the floor and kept it close to his vest on behalf of his people about whom he never spoke. Moss was Jewish. One day, a very typical ethical situation came up about the IRS. Would we shade a disclosure or something of that sort? I responded in a confusing way and Moss thought I was ready to cheat the IRS. He said immediately, "Well that is so hypocritical of you to do all that bible talk and then be so quick to cheat on your taxes." I clarified what I said and we corrected the confusion.

My goal is to encourage you non-believers to emulate the Mystery Moss, to be quick to confront your Christian friends who do these questionable things. Most of the misbehavior in this book was done by Christian people. One of them was fired and locked out of his office. But no doubt there had been ample opportunities for his coworkers to confront him with his dishonest behavior. And that should have happened long before he was caught falsifying government documents.

People of faith need you non-believers to confront us at every turn. Look at these cheats: The original Charles Ponzi was a Roman Catholic. Madoff was Jewish. Shawn Merriman was a Mormon bishop. Allen Stanford was Southern Baptist. Reed Slatkin was a minister of Scientology. And from my corner of the Christian community, John G. Bennett Jr., an evangelical. People of faith are big advocates of the truth that all are sinners. And what proof they offer! If the example we have set means anything, how can we expect any of you non-believers to join us? But the least you could do is hold our feet to the fire with a word of rebuke when appropriate. Any Christian who gets upset and objects to your rebuke is likely not a Christian at all. Feel free to quote me on that; I'll be honored. This is not too much to ask of you non-believers. I hope you will agree.

The sadness I feel at the aforementioned is more than off-set by the good news coming. Allow me to prime the pump for the next chapter, as all writers are obligated to do. And the good news: It is not written by me. It will give you a perspective from a trader who has executed a large quantity of trades from a keyboard for almost a decade. This will most certainly be your environment, and a significant advance it has proven to be.

An old-timer on the floor once told me that about every decade or so, a wild market would replace the old traders with a young, new class of traders. He recalled the crazy market of '62 which retired many. Surely the market of '73 did the same. I came along in a wild grain market fueled by the Hunt family in '77. Then there was the drought of '83 and the crash of '87.

Today we have the biggest transition yet, the move from yelling and screaming to key strokes and fat fingers. And my generation who is being ushered off the floor. How sweet it is.

I have never encouraged or invited my children to join me in this business. And they have shown no interest until recently. Now that circumstances have opened the door for one of our sons to get involved in trading, I have ample motivation to get out of the way and turn things over to a new generation.

The next and last chapter is written by Mark Andrew Ritchie II, not to be confused with me. I have no one to blame for this confusion other than myself. I have tried to encourage the use of the very informal "Mark-the-Greater," and "Mark-the-Lesser." But reception on this distinction has been notably underwhelming. And the way Mark-the-Lesser's trading is going, we will have to reverse it soon anyway.

So if the Liar-Liar section was a bit of a downer, weep not for me. Instead, check this proverb: "A righteous person's father will be filled with joy; yes, he whose son is wise will rejoice in him."[124] In the coming chapter, you will see whereof I speak.

---

[124] Prov 23:24

CHAPTER EIGHT

PRACTICAL AFTERTHOUGHTS
BY MARK RITCHIE II

When people find out I'm a trader, and if they know anything about the industry or my last name, they falsely assume one of a few things. The first of which is that I must be a multimillionaire trader because of my father's or uncle's successes. Secondly, they assume I must be heir to some of the great 'secret sauces' that have produced said wealth for others in my family.

I was once at a seminar for traders where I made the mistake of wearing the name tag they gave me. One guy started a conversation with, "Hey, you know you have the same name as some legendary trader, who I think has written a book or two?"

"Yeah, I've heard that," was all I could think of in response. I could probably tell half a dozen stories like this over the last few years. Worst of all is the fact that my father decided to give me the same first name. So I've been mistakenly credited with writing books in addition to having money and trading prowess. Those, of course, would be the good things I'm mistaken for. I'll leave out the rest for the sake of time. All this to say that when I decided to get into this business, I should have started by looking for a bigger set of feet to fit the proverbial shoes I'd be trying on.

I got my start working for a former associate of my father's about eight years ago. I had really no idea what I was getting into at the time and knew almost nothing about actual trading, nor did I know the spectacularly terrible fashion in which my first endeavor into trading would end. What I can share is some wisdom I remember getting from my father at the start. It has not been spelled out in the previous pages and it could be timeless.

The conversation went almost exactly like this:

"Dad there's something I don't understand about the whole business of trading."

"Yeah what's that?"

I said, "Well, they say that ninety percent of traders wind up losing money. That must mean that only a small fraction of traders actually make any money."

"That's not true at all."

"Well the statistics might be off a little, but it's supposedly a pretty high number."

"In my opinion," he said. "One hundred percent of traders make money."

"What?!?! How's that even possible?"

"If you aren't making money, eventually you won't be trading. So the people in the ninety percent aren't real traders, because real traders make money."

I didn't realize it then, but that last statement would become the philosophical underpinnings of how I look at speculation. What's ironic was that the situation I went into ended so poorly because of the simple fact that the gentleman for whom I was working was not making actual money. In the end, you can boast about your analysis, your entries and exits, how you outperform a benchmark or manage risk till you're blue in the face. But if you aren't making money, the only person you'll fool is yourself.

I'll let the implications of that dialogue hopefully reshape your thinking the way it has mine and give a few more afterthoughts that relate to what I do as a trader.

I don't know what it was like to trade on the floor, because I never have. I don't know what it was like to trade off the floor when you had to phone orders in, because I never have. My Dad has taught me almost nothing about the soybean complex or the soybean crush that he traded for over a decade. He's taught me nothing about pricing option volatility that the firm he helped found was famous for trading. He's taught me almost nothing about the occasional special situations, trading in bank stocks, which is the only real trading he's been doing for the past two decades.

What I can tell you is that he taught me important lessons about how to reason and think, lessons which have had drastic implications on my personal and professional life, such as the dialogue I just shared. Furthermore, when it comes to trading, what he did teach me was how to make sure you won't go bust by trading too big, or won't leave massive profits on the table by trading too small. This meant using what he called his "invest formula," renamed the RR for this book. That's been engrained within me along with some of the principles that it requires.

A few years back, when the subject of an app or doing some writing or speaking on this topic came up, I was pretty skeptical and I said, "Dad, you know now within most trading circles that formula is widely known. So you won't be teaching anything new to any trader worth his salt." A discussion ensued by which he learned that the 'Kelly criterion' or 'optimal f' functions were readily available in many software and research packages. I learned that he wasn't aware that the 'Kelly criterion' was the actual name of the formula.

He said, "I knew this was in a math text book somewhere, but no one in my day was aware of it." So I asked when and where he had come up with his version, and he said, "I wrote it myself sometime in the early 80s."

This is a fascinating example of the old adage, 'necessity is the mother of invention.' The fact that it already existed is irrelevant, because in this example the very creation itself was needed and put to immediate use in the harshest of environments, the free market. In contrast, it's been said that Kelly never once used his own formula in the real world. Sad as that may be, this is how many of life's great discoveries or revelations unfold. Da Vinci, Cayley, and others wrote about the possibilities of aeronautical flight generations before the Wright brothers had the guts to attach glider wings to their bicycles at Kitty Hawk. Ben Franklin tied a key to his kite which got hit by lightning, and discovered the powers of electricity a century before men like Tesla and Edison came along and learned how to harness it—better yet, in Edison's case, profit from it. It's not every day that you get an opportunity to stand on the shoulders of another man's work and continue to profit from it. And in the case of Kelly, you still can. I'm saying this now to all traders or wannabes: If you think you have a good trading idea, put it to work using some of the things taught previously. Kelly can have the name—you and I will keep the profits.

Now as I alluded to and was stated in the earlier pages of this book, there is no 'secret sauce' or 'holy grail.' However, I do think there are implicit values to trading and speculation beyond the formula itself which come into play when applying it. For starters, in order to effectively use this approach, it implies that you have some good baseline assumptions, such as your average win and loss expectations as well as your overall percentage of winning trades. These assumptions can only be accurately arrived upon by traders who diligently track their trades. In this, there is a wealth of information as well as the discipline involved in staring one's trading results straight in the eye.

In my brief career, I've been amazed at how many wannabe traders who've sought my advice (remember because of my last name they assume I'm either a millionaire or holder of said secret sauce) who don't track their trades. The amazing part is that they can't seem to figure out where they're going wrong, yet they don't track their trades. For the sake of argument, let me give one example. I met a guy at a trading seminar to which

I was invited. We connected, and after a period of time he explained that he wasn't having a good deal of success. I had told him that if he spent 90% of his time studying his trades and 10% of his time studying his charts and entry criteria that he'd be better off. So I asked him if he was tracking his numbers. He was reluctant at first to share, but had been doing so upon my earlier advice.

After looking at them, he had a 50% win rate and was winning about 5% on his wins and losing about 5% on his losses. He was almost embarrassed to show these results to me. I, on the other hand was very positive and informed him he was doing a great job, both in tracking his trades and in about two thirds of his trading as well. He was shocked I was so positive about it, but I stated that he only lacked one key ingredient, which his numbers were teaching him, and he now has a choice of how he could fix it. He either needed to up his win rate, cut his losers quicker, or hold his winners longer. If he can could do any one of those three, then he'd be successful. After some discussion, he said that he didn't think he was going to be able to cut his losers or increase his win rate substantially. However, he did feel he could hold onto winning trades longer. I suggested that since he was doing a good job cutting losses, he had to hold his winning trades until they were at least 2x the size of his average losing trades. He took my advice, listened to his own numbers, and has been profitable ever since.

Now there are probably many of you thinking that this example doesn't exactly appeal to using the RR formula itself. However, you can't begin to make any good assumptions with the formula if you have no idea what your trading expectations are, and you have no idea of meeting any expectations if you don't diligently track those numbers. I realize that many are still not convinced, so I'll give you an example from my own experience.

A few years back, I decided to try trading for myself. Initially, I had five ideas to which I allocated amounts of capital based upon my degree of confidence and the numbers I calculated using the RR. The idea I had the least confidence in was some short term trading I was doing in futures. So I gave that idea 10K thinking it would most likely go nowhere. To my surprise, at the end of the first year the strategy was up over 100 percent. After comparing its performance to the other strategies I was trading, I gave it an additional 12K. Since that time, I have not added any money to this approach and only taken profits from it. As of a little more than four years later, it has netted over a million in trading profits. To this day, I shake my head in disbelief how an approach I didn't believe in has done so well. Needless to say, I'm not arguing with the numbers, and the approach has become a staple within my portfolio.

To those who have read this far, and still criticize this book for not revealing or teaching anything new, all I can say is that you "have received your reward in full." That quote should be saved for the FYX sections, but for the person looking for some set of magical rules or the proverbial goose that craps gold, all I can say is, you're seeking the wrong thing and everyone usually gets the reward which they seek. They just might not like the reward.

MY ATTEMPT AT FYX

I was once asked by another trader what books I had read to help me with my trading psychology, or if I had any to recommend. After some time, I shared that I had read many great trading books which far and away helped me improve the way I think about markets and my trading approach. But there was another book that I read that has by far and away had the greatest influence on the entirety of my life. It has helped shape who I am personally, emotionally and spiritually. Of course, you probably realize that I was talking about the New Testament; and this was a completely new idea to him.

I just explained that I think Jesus was the greatest teacher and understood the human condition better than anyone. At that point he already had a good deal of respect for me, so I challenged him to read a few of the Gospels with an open mind and see if there wasn't any wisdom in what Jesus said. Then later, after reflection, I asked whether he thought Jesus was just a wise teacher or a personal savior. He eventually concluded both were true.

One of my favorite pearls of trading wisdom is, "Never underestimate small gains compounded over time." I'm actually not completely sure where this quote came from but I believe it's from Gerald Loeb who was one of the founding partners of E.F. Hutton in the 1920s and wrote the book, *The Battle for Investment Survival.*

Whether he said it exactly isn't as important as the lessons gleaned from his story and the quote itself. The stock market crash of 1929 and the depression of the 1930s had a huge impact on Loeb's overall philosophy. He abandoned the approaches to the stock market that he felt were too risky. He favored smaller gains, shorter holding periods, less margin than were customary in his day. The interesting thing is the writer of Proverbs came to the same conclusion a few thousand years earlier saying, "Whoever gathers money little by little makes it grow".[125]

Both writers realized that taking too much risk on one shot isn't wise. It is funny how much wisdom one can gather through hardships, and this is also a biblical theme. Read the book of Job and you'll find a man who endured quite a crash and depression in his own life and reemerged with incredible wisdom and favor from the Lord.

A second point is one that Mark Minervini has made on the topic of emotions. Mark says that most losing traders live between two emotions: Fear and regret. The inability to pull the trigger at the right time, with the right size, in the right market, are all forms of fear. The emotions after you're in or out of woulda, coulda, shoulda are all forms of regret; these wreak havoc on your confidence and ability to think clearly. I think Mark is on to something bigger—can anyone say they haven't battled fear or regret to some degree?

The good news for Christians is that the number one command from scripture is that we are not to fear. I won't quote where this is in the bible, because it's everywhere. Isn't it ironic that a God would know our basic emotional struggle and remind us where our ultimate hope and trust should be? As for regrets, the cross symbolizes the abolishment of all past, present, or even future behaviors for which we'll have regrets, foolish trading decisions included.

Many skeptics will say that religion or faith isn't necessarily bad, it just happens to be beneficial fiction. Another friend of mine actually claimed that my faith was just putting me in a solid state of mind which allowed me to succeed, but nothing more than just that, a state of mind. I'm not going to argue against these ideas directly, as was done in the previous pages, but there is nothing like the practical world to put these opposing world views to the test.

We will never be able to completely eliminate either of the previous said emotions from our trading or our life. But if our

---

[125]Prov. 13:11

faith provides a solid foundation by which we have the ability to lose things of great value like money, relationships, health, to name a few, then we won't be shipwrecked like the Apostle Paul. He stated, when hardships arose, that we are at an incredible advantage, or in biblical terms, blessed. One thing believers and skeptics should agree upon is that in life and trading, hardships aren't a possibility, they're a certainty. The only question is, who is left holding the fictitious raft, and I'll leave that for the reader to decide.

WELCOME

One day I was in sitting in a lounge just off the trading floor. I have no idea why, but a long-time veteran trader, the owner of Alpha Trading, took the only spot left, the seat next to me. From where we sat, we could still see the quote screens rising two and a half stories above the floor. I had a few years of confidence under my belt at that time. But I was still young enough to see Everett Klipp as a monument to long-term success. At my age then, we never thought we would get to Klipp's age. I'd been at the CBT just long enough to know that even legendary traders don't intimidate anyone. So I said, "Hi, Everett."[126]

Everett Klipp looked, walked, and acted like my uncle Russell. My Uncle Russell was an Eastern Oregon wheat farmer. Uncle Russell's '57 Packard could go 0 to 60 in five minutes, and that was only when he was in a hurry. But an Eastern Oregon wheat farmer is never in a hurry. Plus he never gets the crop in late. Never.

I'd seen Everett around the floor. Every time I saw him I could only imagine him wearing my uncle's overalls. He wore

---

[126] And there's another thing you learn your first day on the floor. I never heard the word "Mister." Everyone is first name. If there ever was a person who deserved respect, it was Mr. Everett Klipp.

the mandatory coat and tie, but his persona made one imagine that he was wearing overalls and had come from the farm for a visit.

Klipp was known to be willing to take any trader's losses in the corn pit as long as those losses were no larger than a quarter of a cent, the minimum tick. He claimed that any trader could make money if they would only take their losses immediately.[127] I have no idea how many floor traders Everett recruited this way. I knew one. He claimed it worked.

So I'm cool (I say to myself). I wasn't going to be intimidated. Plus I already told you that great traders do not intimidate. He was later dubbed the Babe Ruth of the CBT.

I had never met Everett, never traded with him, and never even crossed his path. I guessed he was a corn specialist, a pit in which I never traded. But I knew his son, a trader in my generation and in the pits I traded. He was a wild trader; he could easily dominate the market with his orders. One could always anticipate some excitement when he was in the pit.

So I made a little small talk asking Everett about his son. That was thirty years ago and I have not forgotten his response.

Everett said, "Mark, every order you place must have a stop. The stop goes in with the order." His response was off topic, slightly at least, but maybe not. I sat transfixed as I got a 10-minute summary of the lecture for which Everett I-love-my-losses Klipp had become famous. With the distant sound of the pits in the background, Everett spun out common sense that was almost too common. "I love my losses. I hold my losses. I take my losses."

His response was oblique. I felt a fatherly, almost longing tone in his voice. Maybe he thought I was too young to understand that he had built diligence and patience into his trading style. But I got it. And what I got from Everett in that lounge

---

[127] It's never too late to review the numbers. Suppose Everett was a big corn trader, 100 lots per trade. A quarter cent loss on 100 corn would be $1,250 (one tic is $12.50, times 100). If he were risking a million, that would be about a tenth of a percent (.125) of his capital on each trade.

just off the floor that day is what I've been trying to pass on to you.

Now as I sign off, it occurs to me that it may be fruitful to take another look at the failures of our business to see if they share anything in common. After going through the exercise of the last seven chapters, there may be a common thread. We mentioned earlier that I only knew of two traders who went belly up.

Actually, I've seen far more than that go broke, but the people going broke weren't real traders. They were wannabes posing as traders. And what did they want to be? One might guess, and it's only a guess, that they wanted to be some stereotype of the alpha male, hot shot, Wall Street stud, Michael Douglas. And they are too blind to see that success in this business looks far more like those men in overalls: my Uncle Russell and Everett Klipp.

Here's the problem. You must know if it is *your* problem. No one wants to emulate Everett Klipp anymore—or my Uncle Russell. My uncle never drove his '57 Packard to Chicago. He could not have accelerated fast enough to get down the on-ramp and merge into traffic. Who wants that for a reputation? In this country, this century, this generation, there is not a lot of bragging rights to becoming a millionaire; you have to do it before you're thirty.

Ed Seykota is known for the line, "Everyone gets what they want out of the market." Confused? What he meant is that those who are looking for an adrenaline rush get it. But the end of that road is not pretty. Seykota also said, "The trading adrenaline does diminish over time and with experience. The objective is to rid yourself of it totally."

Ask yourself a simple question and do not lie: Are you willing to have the legacy of the late Everett Klipp, or my late Uncle Russell? If you are so willing, get pencil, paper, and overalls. Because you just may have what it takes to do well in our business. Welcome.

Reaction to the *New Market Wizards* interview:

After reading Jack Schwager's explanation of Mark Ritchie's trading system, I was afraid that Ritchie's interview in *The New Market Wizards* was going to be a little too compacted for me to get much value from it. That couldn't have been farther from the truth. This was one of those interviews where I couldn't stop highlighting one line after another...

Top ... Quotes From Market Wizard Mark Ritchie:

"Lots of people in this business who pass themselves off as successes are really failures. I know one person in particular who to this day writes articles in industry publications and is often quoted by the press, yet he hardly knows the first thing about successful trading." – Mark Ritchie

I think this actually applies to most areas of life. I have discovered that, as a general rule, anyone who feels the need to tell you how successful they are isn't really all that successful. While the technology wasn't developed yet when this interview was recorded, this quote certainly could apply to people who discuss the stock market on Twitter. There are some brilliant traders who are happy to provide insight, and there are some people who have no clue what they're talking about. Your job is to learn how to tell the difference.

"I have a rule ... if I find myself praying about a position at any time, I liquidate it immediately. That's a sure sign of disaster. God is not a market manipulator. I knew a trader once who thought he was. He went broke – the trader, I mean." – Mark Ritchie

This is a thought we have seen previously from other Market Wizards. If you are worried about a position to the point that it keeps you up at night, there is no possible way that you can clearly assess any aspect of the position. The best solution at that point is to liquidate the position. I thought Ritchie's take on this was humorous.

Andrew Selby, *"Don't Talk About Your Stocks"*

Reaction to *God in the Pits*

Excellent ...   **Donald Trump**

... I read about 30 books a year. None has gripped me more.... Must read for seekers of value, truth, and reality in the biggest sense.

Merrill J. Oster,
Publisher, *Futures* Magazine

...the public clamor for insights into the minds of successful traders has placed books such as *Reminiscences of a Stock Operator* among the bestsellers of all time. *God in the Pits* deserves to join it.... A dynamic and well written book— a true page-turner.

Barron's

Makes a case that it is possible to go long on soybeans without compromising one's religious devotion."   **Forbes**

Ritchie seems to have managed the biblically impossible task of serving both God and mammon... On the evidence of his low-key text, which combines a spiritual autobiography and personal memoir with a rags-to-riches success story, he's also an extremely rewarding writer... the author pokes gentle fun at true believers and ideologues...Nor are his oft-expressed views that amateurs should not speculate in commodities calculated to endear him to fellow traders who make fine livings from the public. Another Mark (with the last name of Twain), is said to have remarked on the 'calm confidence of a Christian with four aces.' Ritchie has this sort of assurance and more, which he shares in a very special book.

Kirkus Reviews

... wit and honesty are very appealing. He has a genuine capacity for discerning and conveying spiritual insights—with a refreshing lack of ego inflation...

Library Journal

Some people would be surprised, even skeptical, to hear a trader talk about how he found God and about the importance of God in his life. But that is the story Mark Ritchie successfully relates in this poignant and sensitively written book.

Kansas City Times

... a refreshing breeze blowing across the misty Wall Street world of dog-eat-dog. Every cynic ... needs to read this incredible story ... **Norman L. Geisler**, author, founder,
Southern Evangelical Seminary

Like C.S. Lewis, or Thomas Merton, author Mark Ritchie uses the context of his own life to highlight the incredible spiritual journey he is on ... **Christian Activities Calendar**

Could be just what the pits need. **Institutional Investor**

As a drama of God's persistent presence in life's "pits" I have read few equals ... any human being who has gone through the valley of the shadow of death (or wishes to do a little advance preparation) will be stirred ...

David W. Gill,
President, New College Berkeley

They are ordinary guys and certified psychos, calculating entrepreneurs and seat-of-the-pants gamblers. They are all found in the pits.... Then along comes Ritchie, and you can add Mother Theresa to the stew. Ritchie is a former pit trader and a founding partner of Chicago Research and Trading, one of the leading commodity options trading firms. Unlike most of his peers, the excess baggage Ritchie took to the pits was a fundamentalist Christian upbringing, and even more unlike other traders, he gives his trading profits away to the poorest people in the world.... The effort is something you can pull for, and Ritchie's story is surely one of the most unexpected to emerge from the trading floor ... a true tortuous journey to the promised land.

Chicago Sun-Times Book Review

Reaction to *Spirit of the Rainforest*

Spirit of the Rainforest is a bunch of crap.[1]
Anonymous Anthropology professor, PhD

There is an uncomfortable irony here for us all; that those who are studied might offer their own self-understanding in place of our ethnographies...
Dr. Neil Whitehead, *American Anthropologist*

... one of the most important books of the late 20th century... It should be read by every American and taught in every school.
Theodore Baehr, Television and Film Critic

A master storyteller, Jungleman will draw you into the intense drama of his mysterious people. He takes the reader on a journey that will forever alter our perception of the noble savage.
Dr. Robert Seiple
US Ambassador for International
Religious Freedom

This is a gripping account of the oppressive spirit world of the Yanomami, of their encounters with western traders and anthropologists ... raises important questions that we must answer.
Dr. Paul G. Hiebert
Professor of Anthropology
Trinity International University

... a graphic portrayal of the dynamic transformation of a barbarous tribe ... gut-wrenching and inspiring ... drives a penetrating nail into the anthropological coffin of the leave-the-noble-savage-alone myth.
Dr. Norman L. Geisler
President, Southern Evangelical Seminary

---

[1] Ed. Ritchie claims to love the one-star review, Cf, page 147

ADVANCE REACTION TO
MY TRADING BIBLE

"In My Trading Bible, Mark Ritchie achieves a rare combination making a useful book also fun and entertaining. This book is incredibly thought provoking and should be included in every trader's library. It's a new book just written, but it reads like a classic."

Mark Minervini, Author,
Trade Like A Stock Market Wizard

"Fascinating and convicting ... the life lessons were spot on."

Gerald Mitchell, pastor,
theologian, amateur trader

1.) It's the best trading book that will never get an award.
2.) Chapter 5 scares me, and I been doing this for years; but people interested in trading should really understand drawdowns.
3.) Page 40, the quote on the Young Ruler Parable is the best sentence I ever read about Christians and trading ...

William Leung, Trader, Shenzhen China

Loved the Market Wizard interview [*New Market Wizards*]
Loved the Ritchie Rule app
Ritchie is a rare person ... a true top risk taker for several decades, not a sales man. His book and $1 RR application will help you understand how to survive in the markets so you will have the chance to eventually find the right strategy (for you) and profit in the long term. Everyone must have both. Every brokerage should give both to their client as a gift.

Konstantinos S.Xeroudakis,
ACSI, Financial Advisor, Greece

Disclosure: Mark Ritchie sent me a copy of the book because of my review of his earlier book "God in the Pits". I gave that book only one star and was quite critical of it. He said that my review in part inspired him to write this one, thus the copy of the new book. The one-star rating on the other book should allay any suspicions that I am a buddy of MR's writing a fluff review.

This is a hard hitting book that tells the home truths about what is needed to succeed in the markets. New traders—who perhaps need it the most—might find it very challenging. It will, I think, repay multiple readings as the trader learns and grows. I certainly wish I had had the book a couple of decades ago. I found it very engaging and had trouble putting it down... deserves to become a classic in its field. I have been trading for over 30 years and read hundreds of books on trading and books this good don't come along very often.

Each chapter also has a supplement for Christians, who are often very confused about wealth, assertiveness and some other issues.

Personally I don't find the author's reasons for his faith convincing. I formed the impression that he has not fully understood the alternative points of view... anyone who promotes the argument from design should gain a good understanding of evolution and genetics by reading textbooks on these subjects. At the same time he is very critical of many religious people and points out that successful trading requires the development of real character, honesty and integrity. Such things do not automatically happen from becoming religious.

Still I will give the author full marks for being as honest as he possibly can and for putting his views out there for all to critique. Overall this material does not detract from the book and often adds extra insight into the thinking of a successful trader.

Tim Josling, Trader, Australia
[Josling's full review is available on Amazon]

Seeing past the clutter, to find clarity in decision making that never wavers from guiding principles, is the vision Mark advocates. This marvelous book has the academic strength needed in business schools, with the practical outlook vital on main street. Commodities is his platform and expertise, but the guidance for business and faith found here tackles the issues challenging every leader.

Dr. Roger Parrott
President, Belhaven University

I'm relatively inexperienced in finances and trading, but Mark Ritchie's, *My Trading Bible*, was a terrific introduction to trading and the secrets of trading success (and failure).
…highly informative guide… provides excellent information, and best of all, it is written in a manner that allows novices, like myself, to understand and follow his formula to success. Highly recommended to anyone interested in getting into trading …

Donna Burgess, author of,
Notes from the End of the World.

… The book's focus is on his prescription for success as a trader, which relies on an understanding of the law of averages, a formula for adjusting trades in response to gains and losses, and a solid understanding of one's limitations, often supplemented by pithy advice: "If you can't stand boredom, go to the casino. It's far less expensive." Each chapter concludes with a section specifically targeted to Christian readers …

Kirkus Reviews

ABOUT THE AUTHOR

Mark Andrew Ritchie grew up in the poverty and strangeness of Afghanistan, the deep south of Texas, and an Oregon-coast logging town. The Vietnam War crystallized his love of rebellion. He became an occupational vagabond—funeral home operative, Chicago Transit bus driver, gambler, long-haul trucker, jail guard, and more. After graduate studies in philosophy of religion, he went straight to the take-no-prisoners financial markets of Chicago. (Everyone in those pits comes from somewhere very different.) It was an unlikely backdrop for launching a career in finance where he became one of four founding partners of CRT, a certified yelling and screaming floor trader, a participant in Schwager's, *New Market Wizards*, and creator of the RR trading app. After traveling extensively in the third world, he did a series of book and lecture tours with an ex-shaman from the jungle of Amazonas. His friend was publicly labeled a "token N-word." (Can't print that here.) He raised five children with his wife, then followed after her dream–working with orphans in Asia where he became immersed in barefoot banking. After hearing the children sing, he founded and directed Voices of Myanmar Gospel Choir, seen on YouTube. Today he is Chairman of the Board of RTM^2, a trading group, and lives near Chicago.

MarkRitchie.Me

Check him out at his website where you are encouraged to leave a comment. Ritchie is especially fond of those with contrary viewpoints, i.e., critics.

Made in the USA
Coppell, TX
09 July 2022

79747566R00105